DATE DUE

MAY 14			
MAY 30			
JUN 12			
MAY 26			

GAYLORD 234   PRINTED IN U. S. A.

PLANET EARTH 2000

PLANET EARTH 2000

Facts On File Publications

New York, New York ● Bicester, Engla

This book was devised and produced by
Multimedia Publications (UK) Limited

Editor Angela Royston
Design John Strange
Production Arnon Orbach

First published in the United States of America by Facts On File, Inc.,
460 Park Avenue South,
New York, NY 10016

First published in Great Britain by Purnell Books

Library of Congress Cataloging in Publication Data

Lambert, David, 1932-
  Planet Earth 2000.

  (Your world 2000)
  Includes index.
  Summary: Examines current environmental problems
around the world, their causes, and possible solutions.
Also discusses new sources of energy and minerals and
ways of making our planet a cleaner and better place to
live.
    1. Science--Juvenile literature. [1. Pollution.
2. Environmental protection] I. Asimov, Isaac, 1920-
II. Title. III. Series.
Q163.L28 1985   304.2   84-21155
ISBN 0-8160-1153-2

Printed in Italy
10 9 8 7 6 5 4 3 2 1

CONTENTS

Foreword

There are several million different kinds of living things that share this planet with us. But of all of them human beings are by far the most important because they are the brainiest. They have the ability to do almost anything they want on Earth. They can kill off dangerous competing plants or animals, and protect those plants and animals they find useful. They can dam rivers, steam across oceans, build enormous cities – and so on, endlessly.

But with power comes responsibility. We can improve the Earth for ourselves, make our homes more comfortable, our food more plentiful, our lives safer, but we can't always be sure we're doing that just because it *seems* we are.

We can certainly make our homes warmer by burning a lot of coal, but what if the smoke and soot poison the air and make us ill? We can grow vast crops so that none of us need go hungry, but what if we carelessly destroy the soil in doing so? There may be no crops in some future time. We can increase our numbers and crowd out other kinds of creatures, but what if it turns out that we need those other creatures?

In this book we discuss how human beings, especially in the last few centuries, have been changing the face of the Earth – and not always for the better. In some ways, what's happening is very worrisome, but we can't solve problems by pretending they don't exist. In fact, if we want to make sure that Earth stays friendly and kind to human beings, we must look squarely at the dangers and problems that beset us and decide what we are going to do about them before it's too late. There are a number of things that *can* be done, so this is a book of hope as well as of warning.

Isaac Asimov

Introduction

What sort of planet will today's children inherit in AD 2000? Thousands of years ago, people struggled to shape their environment with primitive tools. Today's vast and growing population has the ability to wreak great changes on the Earth. Tropical rainforests disappear under bulldozers that incidentally destroy thousands of species of animals and plants. Deserts spread rapidly as poor land is overgrazed and badly farmed. Unchecked air pollution kills forests in North America and Europe, where the continued burning of large quantities of fossil fuels could shift the climatic zones northwards, producing deserts in today's grain belts and wheat fields in Scandinavia. This book looks at today's problems and at ways of solving them, for instance, new sources of energy and minerals to replace declining stocks, and new ways of making those stocks last longer. Tomorrow's world could be an overcrowded prison or a comfortable home. The difference depends on us and how we use or misuse nature's fragile wealth.

Author: **David Lambert** has written many information books for children. His particular interests are Earth sciences and natural history.

Consultant: **Tom Burke,** the Green Alliance.

CHAPTER 1

Mankind multiplies

Long ago the Greek thinker Heraclitus wrote, 'You cannot step into the same river twice'. In a way this is true, for river water is always on the move. But Heraclitus meant more than that. He meant *nothing* stays the same.

Scientists have proved this is true of the Earth we live on. Huge changes have happened to our planet since it formed from dust and gas 4600 million years ago.

Oceans have grown and shrunk. Continents have collided. Mountains have risen and been worn down again. Meanwhile plants and animals have appeared and disappeared. Thousands of millions of species probably evolved and died out as others took their place.

Such changes still go on, but mostly very slowly. It takes many millions of years for continents to crash together and thrust up mountains. And most species of plants and animals last for two million years or more.

Our age of change

Now, suddenly, some kinds of change are speeding up. In your own lifetime these changes will enormously affect the biosphere. The biosphere is the Earth's thin outer 'skin' of water, soil and air where plants and animals are found. Life thrives nowhere else on Earth nor on any other planet that we know. So what happens to the biosphere, for good or ill, is enormously important to the future of all living things.

Remarkably, the powerful force at work is just one species of animal — ours. Man is a far weaker species than, say, the lion or polar bear, yet no other mammal flourishes so mightily. Once rare savages, now we number billions. The world's human population has multiplied five times in the last three centuries. Between 1950 and the year 2000 the population will probably have doubled again. It is our own fast increasing population that will most affect the future on our planet.

▼ This graph shows how the world's population has grown since 1650 and might grow by the year 2000. Each band width represents 100 million people. Each colour stands for the population of a different continent.

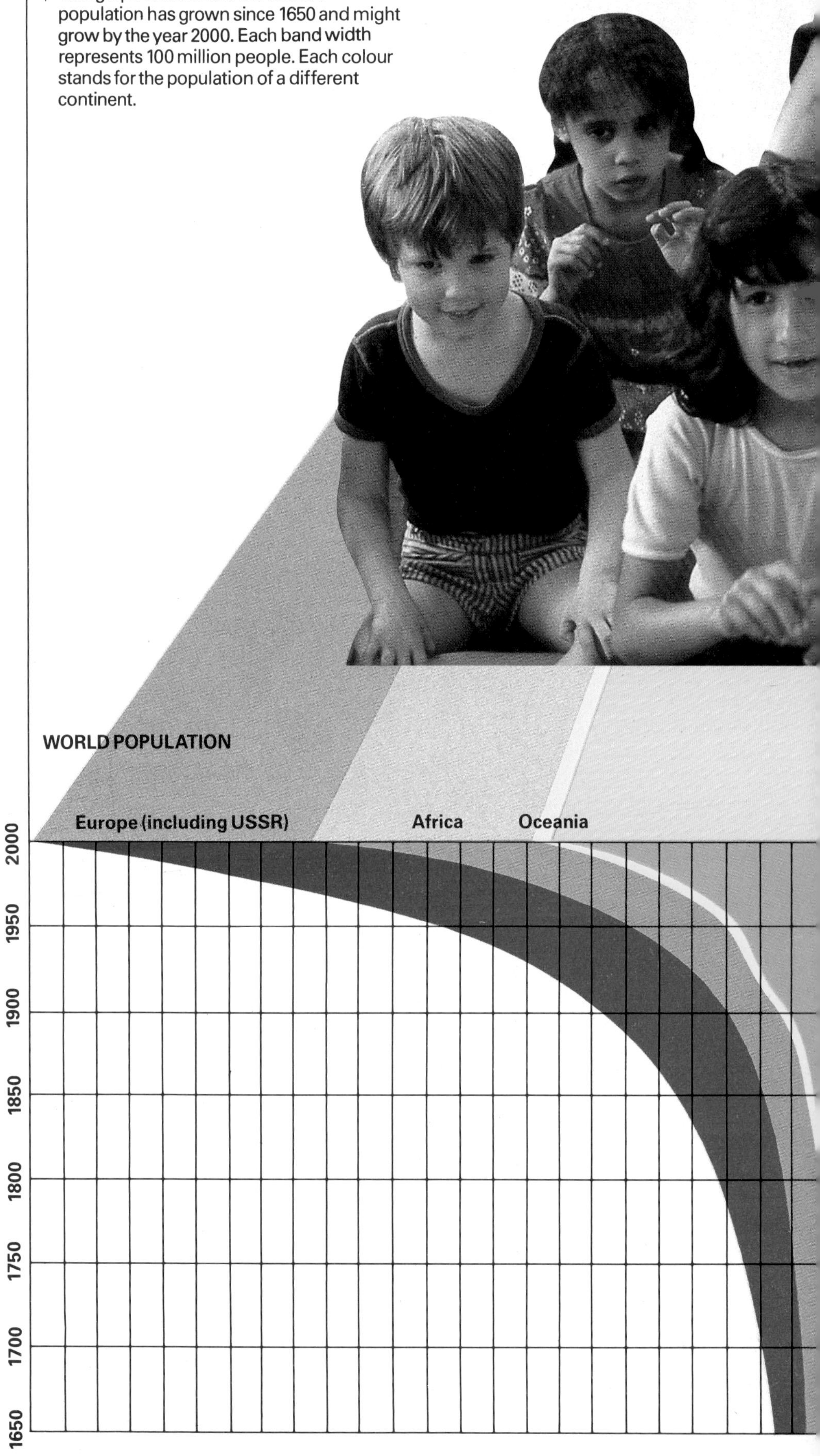

WORLD POPULATION

Europe (including USSR)   Africa   Oceania

2000
1950
1900
1850
1800
1750
1700
1650

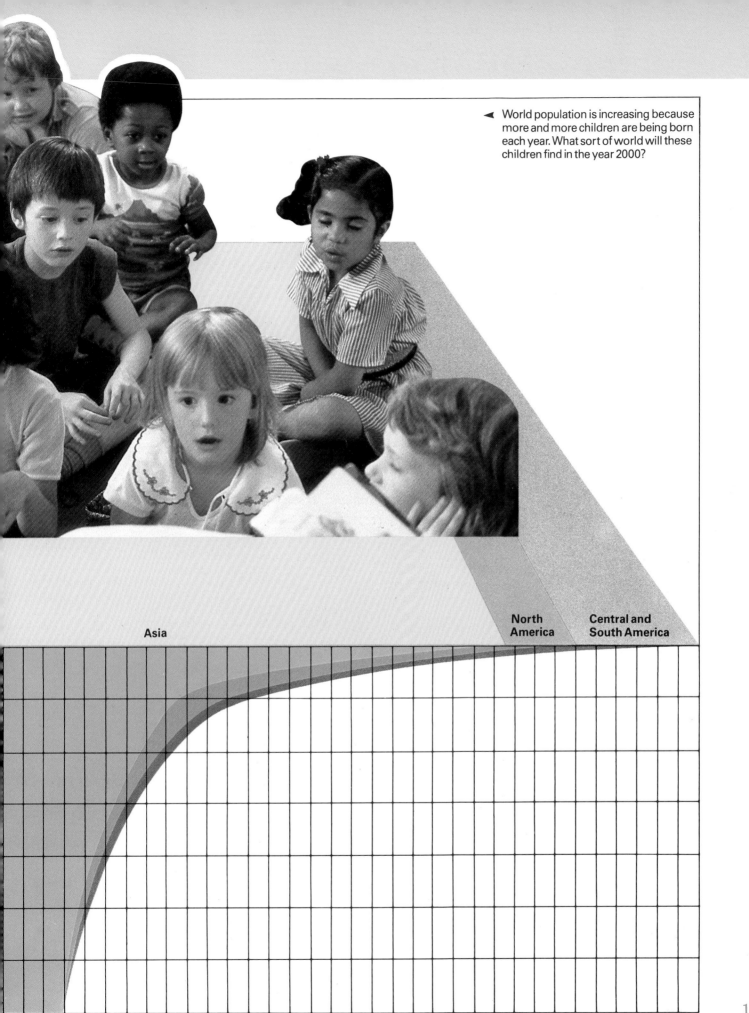

World population is increasing because more and more children are being born each year. What sort of world will these children find in the year 2000?

Asia

North America

Central and South America

Why population grows

The human population is increasing fast today because of the inventions and discoveries of the last four million years.

The hunter-gatherers
Four million years ago, early humans were ape-like creatures, worse off than many other animals. They did not have sharp teeth or claws. They could not outrun a lion, nor even always find enough to eat. Their lives were harsh and very short. There were only a few thousand people in the whole world — all in Africa. Yet even ape-men had important advantages over most other animals. Their forward-facing eyes judged distance well. They stood erect. This freed their hands, which were able to grasp sticks or stones. Above all, early people were brainier than other animals.

By two million years ago, Upright Man had learnt to sharpen sticks and stones for killing prey or digging up tasty bulbs and roots. By half a million years ago these people had discovered the use of fire. This helped some of them spread from Africa to cooler Asia and Europe.

Modern Man had evolved by 40 000 years ago. Cleverer than Upright Man, Modern Man made better stone tools, and spread into the Americas and Australia. Yet, like all Old Stone Age humans, these people depended for their food upon wild animals and plants. Hunters starved if game grew scarce. So by 12 000 years ago there were still only some five million people.

The food-producers
People began multiplying fast only once they could always get enough to eat, by growing crops and keeping animals for food. Farming began about 12 000 years ago, in fertile parts of Asia. By 6000 years ago, farming had helped the world's population to climb to 20 million.

▼

When the Roman Empire was at its height in AD 1, population was about 200 million. In the 16th and 17th centuries, new lands were explored and the spread of food plants helped to feed a world population of around 900 million in 1800. The Industrial Revolution saw a further increase to about 1625 million in 1900, while scientific medicine and farming helped world population exceed 4000 million in the 1970s.

▼

Some of the milestones in population growth. In the Old Stone Age, people still hunted for all their food, and world population was less than 5 million. Agriculture began about 10 000 BC when population had probably reached about 5 million. By 1500 BC cities had grown up and trade with the countryside had increased. The population was then about 60 million.

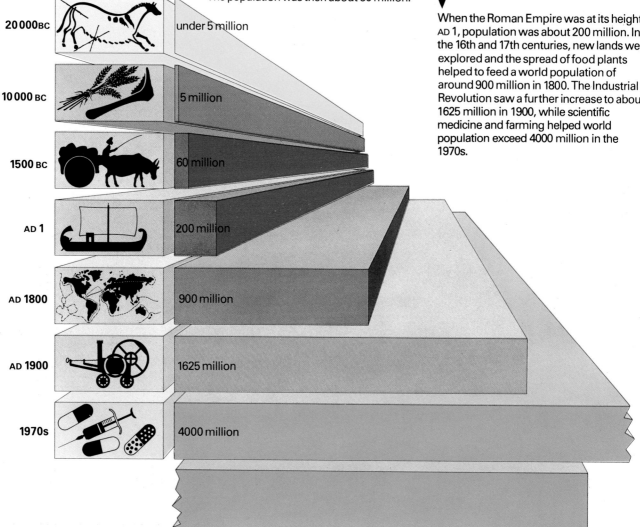

20 000 BC	under 5 million
10 000 BC	5 million
1500 BC	60 million
AD 1	200 million
AD 1800	900 million
AD 1900	1625 million
1970s	4000 million

New inventions such as ploughs and metal tools helped farmers to produce more food than they needed for themselves. They exchanged the spare food with craftsmen who specialized in making tools, weapons and other useful products. Craftsmen built houses close together in early villages and towns. Some towns grew into cities holding thousands of craftsmen, merchants and their families. Manufacturing and trade pushed up the population of cities further still. By AD 1 there were perhaps 200 million people in the world. But much land was still thinly peopled by small bands of Stone Age hunters who had to struggle to survive.

Food from all the world
World population got its next great lift about 500 years ago as European explorers spread their food crops, tools and know-how far and wide. They brought back new plants and food from the lands they explored. Later, millions of Europeans began to settle 'empty' continents like North and South America and Australia.

Since 1800 there have been many inventions, including tractors, harvesting machines, canning, refrigeration, and fast steam-powered cargo ships. Scientists have produced better breeds of crops and animals. There is now more food than ever before and this has helped industry and trade. At the same time scientists have discovered how to prevent diseases that once killed millions of people.

More food means fewer babies starve. Less disease means more people live to reach old age.

Together, these two facts have pushed up populations everywhere.

By 1900 mankind's numbers were already soaring upward like a rocket from its launching pad. That upward flight goes on today even more steeply.

▼

In the Stone Age the pink area of land (representing somewhere in England) was inhabited by 100 people. Today more than 100 people occupy each tiny square shown on the right.

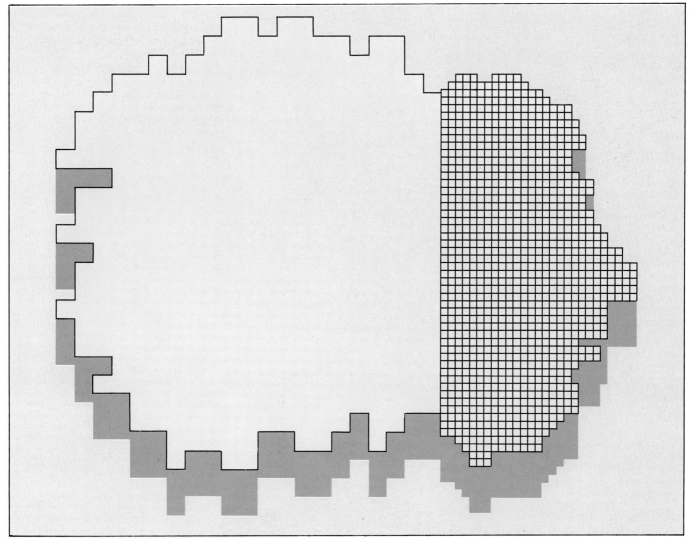

The world remade

The few people of the Old Stone Age made little mark upon the land. Most was untamed forest, grassland, mountain, marsh or desert. Nature ruled people's lives, for big deserts, rivers, seas and mountain ranges were barriers that many people could not cross. Yet the ever-growing number of people and the inventions that helped the population to increase have changed all that.

The more people there are, the more food, water, fuel and other useful substances they need. In time satisfying these needs meant making drastic changes to the surface of great tracts of land.

Putting the land to work

To get more food, people had to grow more crops. This meant they needed extra fertile land. But much of the best soil had a covering of forest. So people began to cut this down. In the last thousand years Europe has lost most of its old forests.

People also won new land by draining swamps and marshes.

▼
The largest earth-movers are higher than Nelson's Column in Trafalgar Square, London, and longer than Wembley football pitch (top). They can move enormous quantities of earth very quickly.

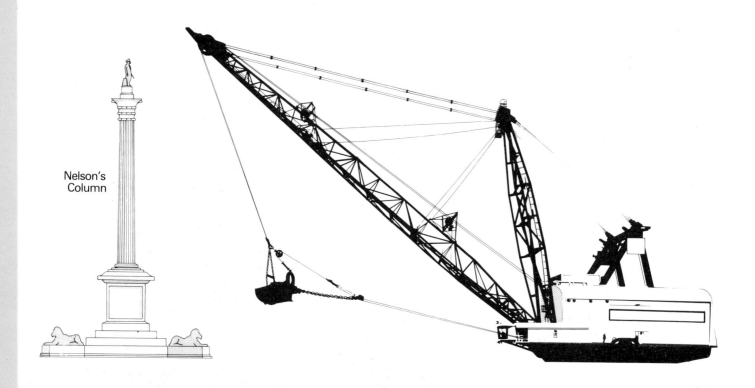

Nelson's Column

14

The Dutch built walls to shut in areas of shallow sea. Then their windmills pumped the water out. Much of the Netherlands stands on land gained from the sea.

New farmland helped feed ever larger cities. As cities grew, their buildings spread across the countryside, on land where plants once thrived. Expanding cities have a growing appetite for fuels like coal and oil and minerals like clay and iron ore for factories to make into useful articles such as bricks and knife blades. So quarrymen and miners dig pits and tunnels or drill deep holes in any land which is rich in useful mineral deposits.

Cities also need transport systems to bring them food and raw materials, and to take out manufactured goods and wastes. So roads, canals, and railways have crept out from cities to the countryside and from one city to another, right around the world. Huge strips of land have vanished under highways made of the artificial rock we call concrete.

Monster muscle power

At first, people had just their own muscle power and that of animals to help them remould the surface of the Earth. So change came only slowly. Now, inventors design great oil-fuelled engines far more powerful than muscles.

One type of dredging vessel can suck up 20000 tons of sand in under an hour. In one day a tractor hauling six ploughshares can dig up over 120 acres (50 hectares). This is enough to grow crops to feed perhaps 240 people for a year. In five days one mechanical mole can drill a tunnel taller than a man for nearly half a mile underground. In less than ten days one giant earth-mover can shift a mass of soil as huge as Egypt's Great Pyramid. This structure may well have taken 4000 men without machines as long as thirty years to build.

Thanks largely to machines like these the rate at which we change the surface of the world is speeding up enormously.

Tomorrow's world

Already grand new plans for change are on the drawing boards. By the year 2000 engineers could reverse the flow of certain Russian rivers to bring water to parched lands in Central Asia. American miners might gouge huge gashes in the Rocky Mountains in their search for oil. Canadians have already started stripping away the topsoil from huge parts of Alberta to extract the fuel-rich tar sands underneath. Looking farther to the future, damming the Strait of Gibraltar could turn the Mediterranean Sea into a shrinking 'pond'. As the level of the sea dropped new dry land could be used around the rim. Once, nature dominated people. Now, people seem to dominate the world. But do we? See the next two pages.

▼

Here in the Soviet Union the Ob and Irtysh rivers flow north to the Arctic Ocean. But in future reservoirs could store much of the water and canals could divert it south to thirsty farmlands and semi-deserts.

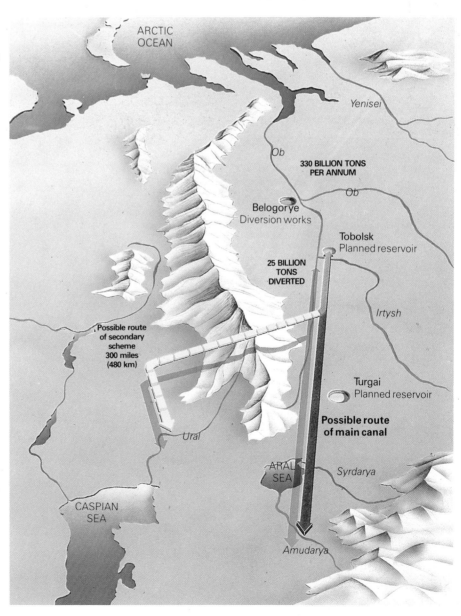

ARCTIC OCEAN

Yenisei

Ob

330 BILLION TONS PER ANNUM

Ob

Belogorye
Diversion works

Tobolsk
Planned reservoir

25 BILLION TONS DIVERTED

Irtysh

Possible route of secondary scheme 300 miles (480 km)

Turgai
Planned reservoir

Possible route of main canal

Ural

ARAL SEA

Syrdarya

CASPIAN SEA

Amudarya

An overcrowded planet

Now we have more power than ever before to make the world provide the food, water, living space and raw materials we need. Yet by the year 2000 many people may be worse off than today. This is partly because the power to shape the world is unevenly spread.

Most power belongs to the people of North America, Europe, Japan, Australia and South Africa — the industrially developed regions of the world. Here, many people work in towns and cities. Many families can afford comfortable homes, with machines that help to banish drudgery from housework, and two cars in the garage. Food is so cheap and plentiful that millions die from diseases due to overeating.

Life is very different in the so-called Third World nations in most of South and Central America, Africa and Asia. Three quarters of all people live here. Most of them have to grow their own food and cannot afford much machinery or other help that might increase their crop yields. In the Third World, hundreds of millions are extremely poor and seldom have enough to eat. If drought or floods kill their crops and cattle, thousands of these people starve.

Reaching the limits

The unequal spread of power and wealth is only half the problem. People everywhere must face up to another: there is a limit to the amount of food and living space that we can squeeze from the surface of the Earth to satisfy our growing numbers.

Take living space, for instance. So many more people will be born between now and the year 2000, that a city the size of London would have to be built every month or so just to house them. But most homes go up on fertile land. So the more houses that are built, the less farmland is left for growing crops to feed the extra mouths. And winning fertile farmland from the wild is not easy because almost all fertile land has been won already.

Homeless beggars crowd temple steps in India. In such poor countries millions cannot earn enough to buy the food they need. This keeps their bodies weak and lays them open to disease.

The same is true of so-called fossil fuels such as coal and oil, and minerals rich in tin and copper. Once used up, these non-renewable resources will be lost to us for ever.

Renewables at risk

Luckily nature renews many of the things we need.

For instance, when a plant is eaten by an animal most of the ingredients of the plant return to the soil in the animal's body waste, and when its body dies and rots. Tiny organisms in the soil turn droppings, dead animals and dead plants into nourishing substances that help new plants to grow. In this way food goes 'round and round' in an unending cycle.

Something similar happens to certain gases in the air. Plants take in carbon dioxide for making food. They give off some oxygen as waste. Animals breathe in oxygen and breathe out carbon dioxide.

Another cycle keeps fresh water on the move: from rain to rivers to the sea, then up as vapour in the air and down again as rain.

But even renewable resources like food, oxygen and fresh water are at risk from the ways in which mankind now tampers with the world. (See chapters 2 and 3.)

Average Daily Food Intake

- More than enough: over 3000 cal/day
- Enough: 2200-3000 cal/day
- Less than enough: below 2200 cal/day
- Details not known

Human lemmings

Unless people at once cut down their appetite for food and raw materials and mend their wasteful, careless ways, the next century could see us suffer a fate like that which overtakes those furry little mammals known as lemmings. When plant foods grow plentiful, the lemmings' numbers multiply until they eat up all the plants around. To avoid starvation, thousands migrate together to find new feeding grounds. There they start a new colony. Unlike lemmings, however, we *have* nowhere to go.

The next chapters explore the risks ahead and how we can and must avoid disaster.

▲
The map above shows the average number of calories consumed by each person in each country every day. Most of the world's hungry people live in the poor nations in the tropics.

▼
As population grows, resources are becoming scarcer. Between 1980 and 2000, the population (shown by the symbol of a person) may increase by half, while the amount of arable land (shown by grain stalks) may decrease by a third and the amount of unfelled tropical forest (shown by trees) may be halved. By 2020 the situation could be even worse.

▲
Each citizen in wealthy Switzerland consumes as much of the world's resources as 40 citizens of Somalia, a poor Third World country.

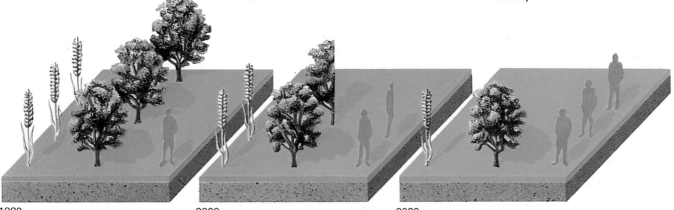

1980   2000   2020

CHAPTER 2
Living landscapes

This chapter explores the great changes happening to landscapes around the world. We start with those man-made landscapes — the croplands.

Bulging breadbaskets

Croplands cover only one tenth of all land, yet they supply most of our food. Can they provide enough as human numbers multiply?

Before 1950 many farmers grew more food by cultivating previously unused fertile land. When the extra land was used up, they increased the amount of food produced by feeding the soil with chemical fertilizers and killing pests with chemical insecticides and chemical herbicides. They dug ditches and laid pipes to bring water to the crops planted in dry soils. They sowed new, heavy-cropping strains of wheat, rice and maize.

Although croplands no longer grew much larger, harvests did. From 1950 to 1970 world grain output almost doubled. From 1970 to 1978 it rose again.

Cropland problems

Now, though, there are signs that farmers cannot go on wringing ever more food from the land.

In places, the area of useful cropland is actually shrinking, particularly in the tropics. Here good land is so scarce that people have to farm steep slopes, dry land or rainy forests. Unless farmers take great care, this newly ploughed soil is quickly washed away by torrential rain or blown away by the wind.

Where wood is scarce, people burn dead plants and dried cow dung instead of using them to fertilize the soil. Deprived of nourishment, their crops fail.

Croplands shrink for other reasons too. If irrigated land is poorly drained, the Sun's heat sucks up salts from deep in the Earth. These salts kill the plants. Half the world's irrigated soils need special irrigation to cure them of this problem.

In the industrial nations, buildings eat up valuable farmland. Between 1975 and the year 2000 new buildings may cover land which could have fed 84 million people.

Other cropland problems threaten the world's food supply. For instance, growing only new, very productive strains of certain crops can be risky. They might be wiped out altogether if their worst pests become resistant to the chemicals we now use to kill them off. In fact between 1965 and 1977 the number of mite and insect species on which pesticides do not work doubled.

Lastly, as the world gobbles up its oil reserves, fuel is becoming

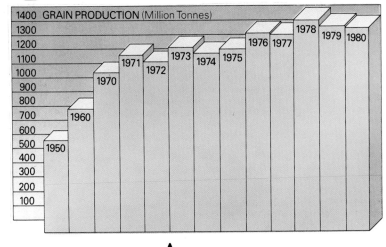

▲ This diagram shows how much grain the world produced between 1950 and 1980. By the late 1970s the yearly harvest had begun to level off.

▼ Nitrogen is an ingredient in proteins – substances that living things are largely made of. Plants take nitrogen from soil. Animals get nitrogen by eating plants. Body waste returns nitrogen to soil, where bacteria make the nitrogen available to plants again. Animals and most plants cannot use the nitrogen in air.

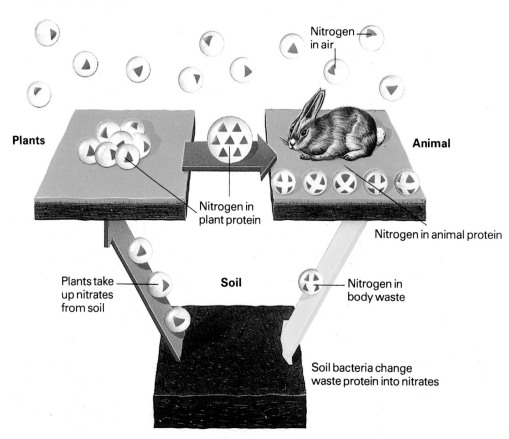

Nitrogen in air

Plants

Animal

Nitrogen in plant protein

Nitrogen in animal protein

Plants take up nitrates from soil

Soil

Nitrogen in body waste

Soil bacteria change waste protein into nitrates

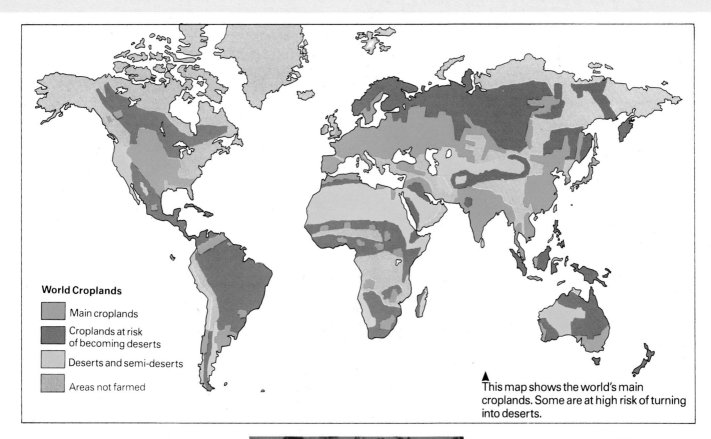

This map shows the world's main croplands. Some are at high risk of turning into deserts.

scarcer and more costly. Fuel is needed to make and power farm machines and produce chemical fertilizer and pesticides. Anyway there is a limit to the extra food that farmers can produce simply by feeding plants with chemicals.

Food for the future
Some experts feel sure that the world need not have run short of

A tractor mows alfalfa. This valuable fodder crop is unusual– it enriches soil with nitrogen obtained direct from air.

food by the year 2000. They argue that governments can persuade farmers to tend their soil more carefully, and scientists will persuade governments to stop building on valuable farmland. Optimists say that scientists will also breed new strains of ever more productive and more pest-resistant crops and animals. Geneticists have already begun tinkering with genes — tiny ingredients in cells that tell them how to grow. Tomorrow's wheat might be made to produce its own nitrate fertilizer.

We could get more food from today's farmland if farmers grew more high-protein plants, such as soya beans. At present much fertile land is used to graze cattle and grow grain to feed to pigs and cattle.

On pages 54-55 we shall look more closely at changes that could help to save the countryside.

Yet even optimists agree that each acre farmed today must feed more than one and a half times as many people in AD 2000 as it fed back in the 1970s.

An African stabs harsh, dry soil in Chad, to break the ground for cultivation.

19

Rangelands

The most abundant nutritious stuff on Earth is cellulose, the main ingredient in leaves. Unluckily for us we cannot digest the roughage in blades of grass or tree leaves. But cattle, sheep and goats all can. By eating their meat and drinking their milk, or turning it into cheese or butter, we get the nourishment in plants at second hand. We get much more besides, for these animals yield wool or leather, and their droppings can fertilize soil or be burnt as fuel.

Cattle, sheep and goats have become enormously important. New Zealand and Uruguay largely depend on livestock for their wealth. In the United States, beef cattle or dairy products provide three out of every five states with their chief source of farm income. In much of Africa nomadic people depend for food on flocks or herds .

▲ The American beefburger depends increasingly for meat on cattle raised outside the United States. Many herds now roam rangelands carved from Central American forests.

Feeding the food animals
As mankind's numbers grow, stockmen try to raise more cattle, sheep and goats to meet the growing need for meat and milk. But larger herds and flocks need

▼ Here in Kenya hungry herds of goats overbrowse the land, killing off already scanty vegetation.

► The world's main grasslands.

extra fodder. The rangelands where most graze or browse are vast, but not unending.

Rangelands of one kind or another take up almost one quarter of the Earth's land surface. (That is roughly twice the area under crops.) They include huge tropical grasslands, called savannas, and much of the world's cool grasslands — Central Asia's steppes, North America's prairies, Argentina's pampas, South Africa's veld, and Australia's downs.

Although rangelands are immense, most of them are too dry or steep for growing crops. Some are very unproductive. A single sheep needs up to sixty times as much grazing land in dry Saudi Arabia as on England's lush, well-watered pastures.

Enlarging the larder

So far, rangelands have helped support a vast increase in the number of cattle and sheep farmed. Between 1950 and 1976 the world's output of mutton rose by half and beef production doubled. Herds of cattle increased fastest in Oceania (including Australia). Goats and sheep multiplied most in parts of Africa and Asia. By the mid 1980s the world held some 3000 million sheep, goats and cattle, nearly half as many again as in 1955.

There are several reasons why this happened. Better medicine helped to protect the beasts from disease. Wells and pipes brought water to cattle in dry lands. Governments helped to stop tribesmen fighting over tribal rights. Herdsmen felled forests to produce new rangelands. Then, too, the Americans, Europeans, Japanese and Russians keep many cattle in small areas by feeding them grain produced on croplands.

Rangelands at risk

By 1980 livestock was no longer multiplying as fast as earlier. Some experts doubt that livestock numbers can ever increase to much higher levels.

The main reason is that many rangelands now have more creatures than they can feed. This happens in India, the Middle East, north-east Brazil, and some other places in the tropics. Dry lands are most at risk.

In places, farmers seize the herdsmen's best lands for growing crops. This forces herdsmen out into ever drier, less productive, land. There, overcrowded cattle quickly eat the tasty grasses, then grow thin and start to die of hunger. For a while, sheep manage on less useful plants. When these are also gone, only goats can eat the tough or prickly vegetation that moves in.

Saving the rangelands

Scientists believe that the best way to save overcrowded rangelands is to curb the size of flocks and herds. But this is easier to say than do.

Another idea is to keep and eat desert antelopes that thrive better than cattle on dry land.

Not everyone is gloomy: in 1978 an American research centre argued that livestock numbers would pass 3600 millions by the year 2000. But this would be largely thanks to extra feed from valuable croplands. Even then the extra meat and milk would not match the rising needs of our growing population. By the year 2000, poorer nations will have even less meat and milk per person.

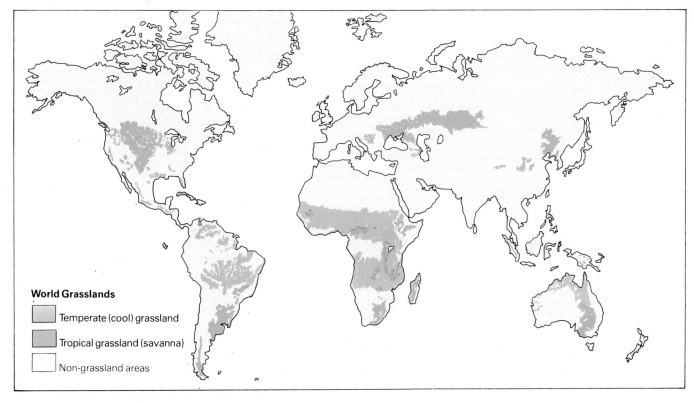

World Grasslands

Temperate (cool) grassland

Tropical grassland (savanna)

Non-grassland areas

Vanishing forests

World Forests

- Boreal (cool) forest
- Temperate forest
- Tropical forest
- Areas with no forest

This map shows the three main types of forest: boreal (mostly conifers); temperate (oak, beech, etc); and tropical.

Forests are immensely valuable places. We can use their wood for building, making paper, or as fuel. Forest plants provide foods, medicines, cosmetics and many other products.

Forests also help us just by being there. On mountain slopes they protect soil from being washed away by rains. Trees also soak up moisture and release it slowly. This helps to produce an even flow of water in rivers.

Trees on the retreat
Forest covered a quarter of all land in 1950. By 1980 one fifth had gone. Much more will vanish by AD 2000, as each year an area of forest as big as Hungary falls under the axe.

The worst losses occur in the tropics. Tropical rainforest has more kinds of plant and animal than any other type of land. But businessmen hire huge machines to clear vast areas. They sell the wood and then plant crops or graze cattle in the clearings.

Poor farming tribes have long grown crops in forest clearings. They moved on when the soil lost its fertility; the soil then had time to recover and support new forest trees. Now, overcrowding means that more farmers clear more land, overwork it, and do not allow it time to recover its fertility.

Between them, businessmen and farming tribes are devastating the great rainforests of Central and South America, South-East Asia and West Africa. These ancient forests could all vanish in a century or less.

Their loss is doing much more than wiping out countless kinds of plants and animals. It is making life harsher for the people who live there. When the soil on mountainsides has no tree roots to hold it, the rain washes it downhill as silt that clogs up reservoirs and rivers. Already, parts of the Panama Canal are too silted up to take large, laden cargo ships.

Without trees to help soil slowly soak up rainwater and release it, mountain rivers tend to flood after rainstorms and dry up in fine weather. In the 1970s floods caused by felling forests in the Himalayan mountains destroyed crops on the plains of northern India. Famine followed and one third of a million people died there.

Saving the forests
At last people have begun to realize that trees are worth protecting. Indian villagers hugged trees to stop them being felled. In Tasmania, Australia's government stepped in to save one of the world's last untouched temperate forests from being drowned by a man-made lake.

Some countries make sure that woodmen replant forests they have cleared. In the 1970s South Korea planted quick-growing pines on huge areas of hillside that had suffered from deforestation. Since 1950 China has more than doubled its forest area by planting lands the size of Italy. But governments must act now if they are to save the splendid forests of the tropics.

◀ Indians burn forest land in Nicaragua. Later they will plant maize and rice among the ashes.

▼

Brazil's Trans-Amazonian Highway cuts a great gash through the world's largest tropical rainforest. Settlers will move in along the road, destroy the forest on both sides, and try to farm the land.

Wetlands

No one much enjoys squelching through a marsh or swamp. Yet its muddy waters teem with plants and animals designed to cope with wet conditions. Some wetlands support more life than almost any other place of their size. No habitat more deserves preserving; yet none is more at risk today.

Why wetlands matter

Wetlands come in many forms. There are inland marshes, bogs and swamps; also coastal estuaries, saltmarshes and mangrove swamps.

Estuaries and salt-marsh creeks are covered with fertile silt washed off the land, and so are far richer in plant foods than the open sea beyond. Wetlands of this kind are teeming nurseries for fish and shrimps.

Among the most productive of these nurseries is the Wadden Sea, an island-sheltered strip that rims part of the southern North Sea. Almost all the North Sea's herrings and more than half its brown shrimps grow up in this shallow, sheltered feeding ground.

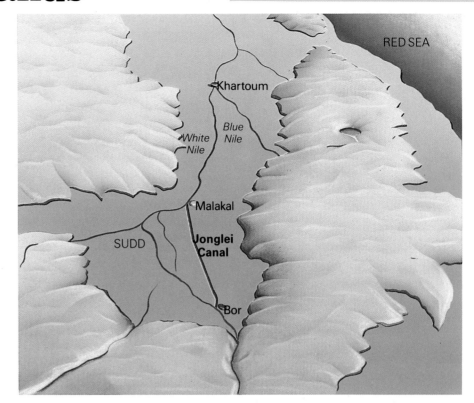

▲ The Jonglei Canal takes White Nile river water on a short cut through Sudan's great swamp, the Sudd.

▼ The Wadden Sea's sandy shores look lifeless at low tide. But billions of living worms and shellfish lurk beneath the surface.

► This bird's-eye view shows a sluggish river wandering across the Sudd. Such snaky waterways dump rich supplies of fertile mud.

24

A huge part of the North Sea fish catch depends upon the Wadden Sea. And a far, far larger catch depends on estuaries in the United States.

Wetlands also serve as giant feeding grounds for birds. Each year waders, ducks and geese feed here by the hundred thousand. Immense flocks migrating from their Arctic breeding grounds stop off to rest or spend the winter on the marshes and mudflats of Europe, Asia, Africa and North America.

Why wetlands disappear
Fishermen, wildfowlers and bird-watchers well know how valuable wetlands are. But farmers, builders, factory owners, shipping companies and yachtsmen believe that many wetlands could be put to better use.

All around the globe, engineers are draining swamps and marshes to make fields and building land, or dredging shallows to make deep-water ports or yachting marinas. At the present rate all the United States' remaining coastal wetlands could vanish in one hundred years.

In Europe, the food-rich Wadden Sea is under several threats. Poisons from the River Rhine have started killing eider ducks and sandwich terns. Plans for chemical factories and nuclear power plants threaten the Wadden Sea with dredging, drainage and pollution.

On the other side of the world, the land-hungry Japanese have reclaimed much of Tokyo Bay and Hokkaido Marshes. Meanwhile Sri Lanka's mangrove swamps dwindle as people cut down mangrove trees for firewood.

Inland, farmers and builders fill in ponds, the homes of countless fishes, frogs and water plants. On a larger scale, drainage ditches are drying out the last great Irish bogs.

But the Jonglei project in the African nation of Sudan is the most ambitious wetland scheme of all. Its huge canal will make a short cut for the White Nile, to stop that river losing water as it meanders through the Sudd, a swamp as big as Wales. Water saved like this might help crops to grow on immense tracts of

land. Also, grasslands would replace swamplands drained of water.

Yet some experts fear that if much of the Sudd dries up, large regions of the area around will suffer from drought.

In fact destroying wetlands does several kinds of damage. It robs us of rich supplies of food and threatens many fishes, birds and other living things. Draining inland swamps removes giant sponges that soak up river water and release it slowly later on. Without these controls the ground around some swamps might turn into a desert when the river levels dropped.

Saving the wetlands
Luckily governments increasingly agree that many wetlands should be saved. A worldwide 'save them' campaign began in 1971 with a meeting in Iran. Ten years later nearly thirty nations had agreed to make wise use of wetlands. Each would set aside at least one to be kept unchanged for ever. Now governments have named over 200 important wetlands, covering in all an area as big as Belgium.

The empty lands

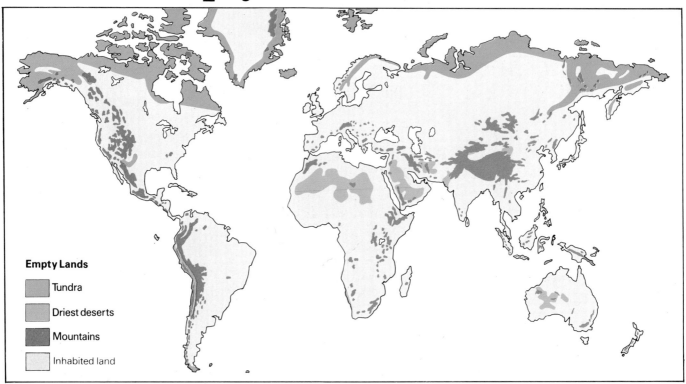

Empty Lands

- ▨ Tundra
- ▨ Driest deserts
- ▨ Mountains
- ☐ Inhabited land

'Empty' lands are those thinly peopled places too dry or cold or steep to yield much food, though some are beautiful and are home to many fascinating plants and animals. One kind of empty land — the desert — is growing at great speed, and to our disadvantage.

Advancing deserts

Vast tracts of barren sand, stones and rock have long sprawled across the dry regions of the tropics and through the heart of Asia. Now, deserts are also spreading fast into the lands around them. Each hour Africa's immense Sahara Desert gobbles up enough country to make a sizable farm. Already four fifths of the world's driest food-producing land is on the way to turning into desert.

Why deserts grow

Deserts spread because too many people try to win a living from the dry lands on the desert rim. Dry, dusty soil just blows away when farmers plough it up for growing crops. The same thing happens when herds of cattle eat all the grasses whose roots hold the soil together. Soil also blows away where people chop down all the trees for firewood. (Wood is so scarce in the Saharan state of Upper Volta that women spend two hours a day just finding fuel to cook the evening meal.)

Many of the people who live in the semi-arid lands of the spreading deserts suffer from famine. Since the early 1960s thousands have starved to death as drought killed off their cattle right across the Sahel — the great belt of semi-desert land lying just south of the Sahara. North-east Brazil is little better off. Life is also harsh

> **Desert growth – The facts**
> Two in three nations affected.
> Deserts now occupy 3 million
> sq miles (8 million sq km).
> Eventual desert area may be 9
> million sq miles (24 million sq km).
> The Sahara expands by 4 million
> acres (1½ million hectares) a year.
> By AD 2000 one third of today's
> cultivated land may be desert.

◀ Gathering fuelwood for this Niger market meant destroying trees and so may be helping the immense Sahara Desert to spread still more.

for millions who scrape a living in north-west India's dusty semi-deserts. Haiti, already very poor indeed, could soon be the first man-made desert in the Caribbean Sea.

Pushing back the desert

Except where climate causes deserts, protecting soil is not that difficult — in theory. In 1977 a United Nations meeting held in Kenya laid plans for fighting back against the deserts. Experts advised that land which is overgrazed by sheep or cattle can recover if it is fenced off and the animals kept out for several years. Afterwards the animals can graze again, but not so many that they eat grass faster than it can regrow. Then, too, drought-hardy sheep are likely to thrive better than cattle on dry land. The problem is how herdsmen and shepherds stay alive while shut out from their pastures.

Bringing water to dry lands helps crops to grow. But good irrigation schemes are costly. It might be best to develop high-yielding strains of millet and sorghum, grains which stand up well to drought. But most high-yielding crops use plenty of expensive fertilizer. Few peasants can afford enough.

One sure and easy way of saving land from deserts is to plant the kinds of shrubs or trees that thrive in arid lands. Acacias and some other trees grow fast and can be used as timber, burnt, or fed to cattle. People are already planting broad belts of hardy, drought-resistant trees around such Sahel towns as Niamey in Niger and Ouagadougou in Upper Volta.

However much is done, though, semi-arid lands may always be at risk from drought.

◄ This map shows the three main kinds of 'empty' lands: deserts, tundra, and mountains.

▼ Four ways of combating the spread of deserts: 1 Irrigation. 2 Ovens and stoves use half as much fuel as open fires.

3 Planting trees like acacias provides shelter and stops the wind blowing the soil away.
4 Plants help to stabilize sand dunes.

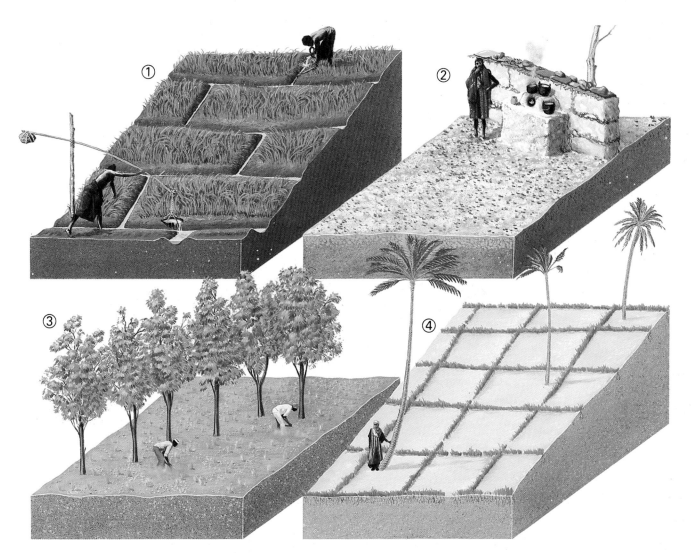

CHAPTER 3
Air and water

Air and water are vital to all living things. Without water you would die of thirst in days. Without air you would suffocate in minutes.

Smog and lead

Air is a mixture of invisible gases — including nitrogen, oxygen and carbon dioxide. Air is polluted when burning fuels give off gases and particles that poison it. Coal and oil are rich in sulphur and are the worst culprits. When they burn they both release sulphur dioxide gas. If that mixes with fog it forms a dirty yellow cloud called smog. Thick smog can be a killer. In 1952, 4000 people died in London in the world's worst air pollution tragedy.

Some smog-hit cities cured this problem by stopping people burning fuels rich in sulphur. But poor countries are less able to afford such laws. By the late 1970s London's air was 16 times cleaner than Calcutta's in India.

But not all smog is caused by sulphur dioxide. In the 1960s Los Angeles in California suffered from a yellow-brown photochemical haze that stung the eyes. Los Angeles has many cars and lots of sunshine. Photochemical haze forms when sunlight acts on nitrogen oxide, a gas produced from the exhausts of cars and trucks. By fitting vehicle exhausts with special filters, Los Angeles has helped to solve the problem.

Car exhausts can cause another danger: lead pollution. Lead in petrol helps car engines to run smoothly, but lead is also poisonous. Breathing in large doses damages young children's brains. To stop this happening, the United States pioneered new laws to reduce the amount of lead in petrol. By the 1990s several other nations will have done the same.

Acid rain

A way of getting rid of some air pollution is by building factory chimneys very tall. Escaping gases are carried away upon the wind. But this takes the trouble to people far away. The gases pollute water

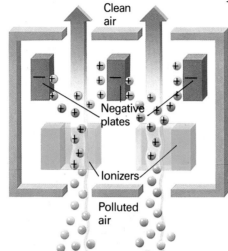

Clean air

Negative plates

Ionizers

Polluted air

◄Electrostatic precipitators are used by factories to clean polluted air. Polluting particles, given a positive charge by the ionizers, stick to the negative plates.

drops in the air, making them into an acid. When it falls this acid rain kills off plants.

By the 1980s acid rain was harming crops in California and New Jersey. It was killing trees in the woods that cover one quarter of West Germany, and was gnawing deeply into many city buildings.

Preventing acid rain calls for

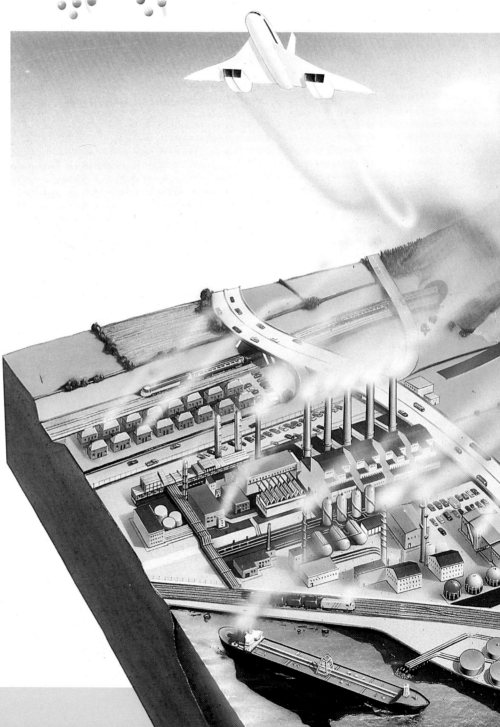

burning fuels in brand-new ways, or fitting filters to clean smoke before it is released. Only rich nations can afford to take these precautions to stop polluting one another's air. So acid rain may still be falling in the year 2000.

Protecting the protector

High up in the atmosphere a layer of the invisible gas ozone shields us from ultraviolet rays beamed down

◄ The left-hand side of this German statue's face was photographed in 1968. The right-hand side was photographed in 1908. The damage came from 60 years of air pollution.

from the Sun. Without that layer of ozone, plants and animals might suffer serious diseases.

Scientists now realize that we are damaging the ozone layer in several ways. The main dangers come from nitrate fertilizers, exhaust gases given off by supersonic planes, and the so-called fluorocarbons used in spray cans and refrigerators.

Only a tiny fraction of all ozone has probably been lost so far. To help protect the rest, countries are reducing their fluorocarbon output. Scientists will keep a close watch to see if we should do more.

◄ Arrows show how pollution is carried away from an industrial area.

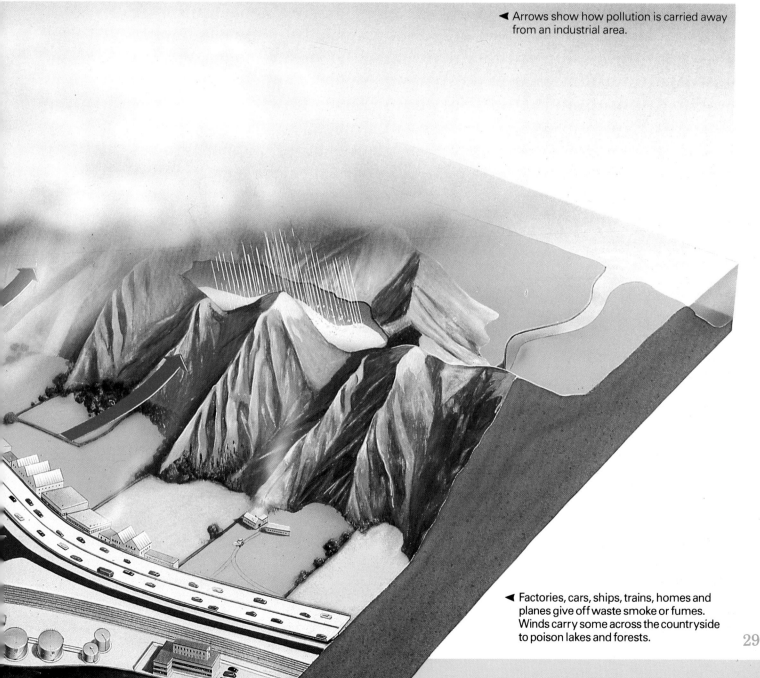

◄ Factories, cars, ships, trains, homes and planes give off waste smoke or fumes. Winds carry some across the countryside to poison lakes and forests.

Changing climates

Some lands, once comfortably warm, lie deeply frozen under ice and snow. Other lands, once deeply frozen, are now mild, warm or hot. Scientists used to think that huge climatic changes like these took many thousand years. Now we know that climates can grow warmer or colder, wetter or drier, in just ten years or so. Indeed large changes in climate may be under way right now.

A warming world

In the 1980s experts predicted years of violently changing weather — droughts, floods, bitter winters and scorchingly hot summers. But by the middle of the next century probably the main change will be a warming up. This could be the first big climatic change produced by people, not nature.

Heat is entering the atmosphere from cars, factories, power stations and homes around the world. But much of this heat leaks out to space. The main reason why the world warms up is different.

Each day billions of people burn huge quantities of wood, coal, oil and gas. Burning produces carbon dioxide gas. So do decaying roots in chopped down forests. In fact more carbon dioxide is entering the atmosphere than plants are taking out for making foods.

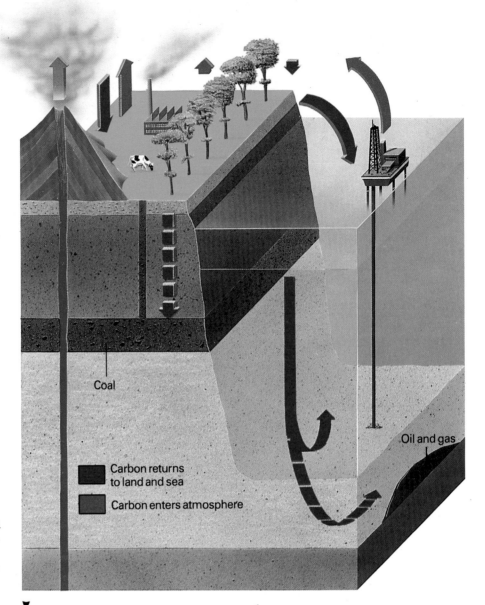

Coal

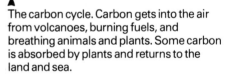

Carbon returns to land and sea

Carbon enters atmosphere

Oil and gas

▼ Ice gripped northern lands for most of the last 900 000 years or so. Another phase of cold seems likely in a thousand years or less.

▲ The carbon cycle. Carbon gets into the air from volcanoes, burning fuels, and breathing animals and plants. Some carbon is absorbed by plants and returns to the land and sea.

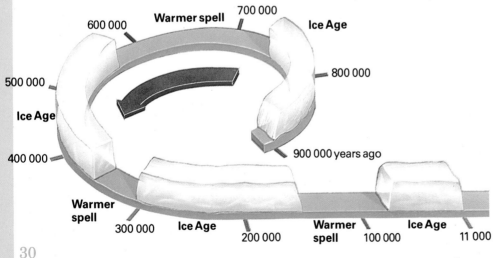

Warmer spell — 700 000

600 000

Ice Age

500 000

800 000

Ice Age

400 000

900 000 years ago

Warmer spell — 300 000

Ice Age — 200 000

Warmer spell — 100 000

Ice Age — 11 000

Carbon dioxide collecting in the atmosphere acts like a greenhouse roof. It lets the Sun's light pass through to reach the Earth. There the light turns to 'heat energy' that tries to escape back into space. But the 'roof' reflects it down again. So heat from solar energy builds up to warm the air near the ground.

This greenhouse effect has already warmed the world a bit

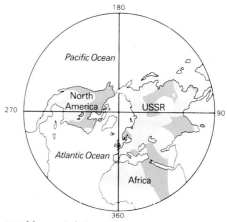

180

Pacific Ocean

North
America
270   USSR   90

Atlantic Ocean

Africa

360

☐ More rainfall
☐ Less rainfall
☐ Not enough information

▲
A man-made rise of carbon dioxide in the air could warm the atmosphere and make some places rainier and others drier than they are today.

◄ New York might look like this if the world warmed up enough to melt ice caps and so raise ocean levels.

since 1965. Now that warming process is accelerating.

The effects could be remarkable. Deserts could migrate toward the polar regions. Crops could fail across the great grain lands of North America, but wheat would grow in chilly northern Sweden. The world's great ice caps would begin to melt and the sea level to rise. After a hundred years or more, the oceans could overflow, drowning many great cities.

We could help to prevent this by simply planting trees wherever forests have been felled. Trees would help 'mop up' enough carbon dioxide to slow down or stop the warming process.

A new ice age

Although the world is warming up today, it could plunge swiftly into a new ice age. Indeed experts say we are living in a short warm phase inside the ice age that began two million years or so ago. The next cold phase might come quickly if an asteroid hit the Earth or if there were a vast volcanic eruption. Either could throw up a cloak of dust that would shut out much of the Sun's heat and light.

As the world cooled down, mild climates would become severely cold. Ice and snow would cover northern North America and Europe. People would flock into the still warm tropics. Overcrowding

would bring wars and famine. The world's population would shrink to a bare fraction of what it is today.

At least one scientist thinks we might prevent all this. The British astronomer Sir Fred Hoyle argues that the answer is to store up enough heat in the oceans to keep the world warm until the dusty atmosphere has cleared enough to let the Sun shine brightly again.

Hoyle's plan involves pumping up deep, cold, ocean water to be warmed by the sunshine. But this scheme would take 2000 years or more. Let's hope the next ice age will wait that long.

Rivers and lakes

The world's stock of fresh water is immense. But most is locked up in ice. Less than a quarter lies on the Earth's surface in rivers and lakes, or underground.

In 1980 people 'borrowed' one tenth of the water from these sources. We used the water for drinking, washing, watering crops, and farm animals, and supplying factories and power plants.

By AD 2000 we may be extracting seven times more water than in 1980, to meet our multiplying needs. Even this would use up only half of the supply, and most of that would find its way back into the rivers, lakes or rocks. Yet in places water is already scarce and will grow scarcer.

Winning water

Engineers can end some local water shortages. One way is to dam rivers to make man-made storage lakes, then pipe the water overland to distant farms and cities. The largest artificial lakes are vast: Ghana's Lake Volta is almost as big as the island of Cyprus.

Engineers can also drill wells and boreholes to reach water trapped in rocks deep underground. In one Nigerian village a new well means that it now takes half an hour rather than two days to gather a week's supply of water.

Taking extra water from the ground causes trouble if people remove it faster than nature can replace it. For instance, near Phoenix, Arizona, groundwater levels are falling by 16 feet (5 metres) a year.

Also, more water for cities can mean less for croplands. So how to share shrinking supplies may be a problem. Some towns may have to bring in rationing.

New sources of fresh water may help. Already some Arab states process sea water to remove the salt. One day, icebergs towed from Antarctica might provide extra water for thirsty California.

Poisoned waters

We need not just enough water, but enough of the right kind. Yet homes, farms, and factories are poisoning the lakes and rivers.

Untreated sewage pours into some lakes and helps bacteria to multiply. These bacteria use up the oxygen in water, so fish suffocate. Also anyone drinking water containing germs from sewage may suffer serious diseases like cholera or typhoid. Much of the world's disease comes from drinking contaminated water.

Insecticides, herbicides and fertilizers are washed off farmland by the rain and pollute countless streams. Poor irrigation methods poison the soil with salt. This way farmers lose maybe as much cropland as they gain by watering the arid lands.

Mines, factories and power stations pollute rivers with chemicals and hot water. Factory chimney fumes produce acid rain now killing fish and plants in thousands of lakes in Canada, the United States and Scandinavia.

The clean-up

Already, though, some nations have begun to clean up inland waters. The Scandinavians add lime to their lakes to free the water from unwanted acid. Filters remove harmful chemicals from the factory waste poured into rivers, lakes or air. Sewage treatment has made London's River Thames fit for salmon to swim in for the first time since the 1830s.

Sadly, water treatment is not cheap. By AD 2000 only rich nations may be able to afford as much clean water as they need.

▼
Foaming or discoloured rivers are often signs of water poisoned by detergents or other chemicals.

▼
[Inset top] Spraying lime treats acid-poisoned lakes, allowing fish to live in them again.

[Inset below] Water treatment plants purify polluted water and make it fit for us to drink.

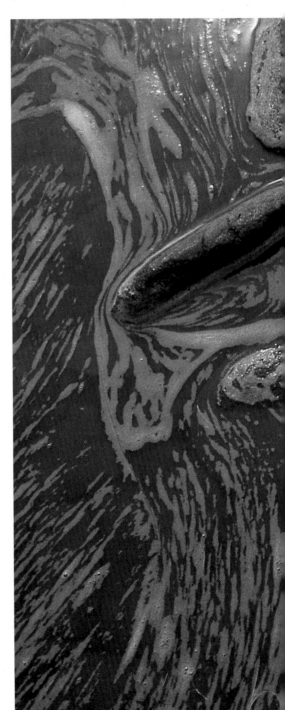

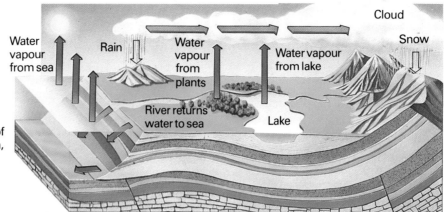

The water cycle. The Sun's heat draws up water vapour from the sea to form clouds of droplets. This water may fall on land as rain, hail or snow. It waters the plants and runs into lakes and rivers and eventually drains back into the sea. The water cycle provides a constant supply of fresh water.

Seas and oceans

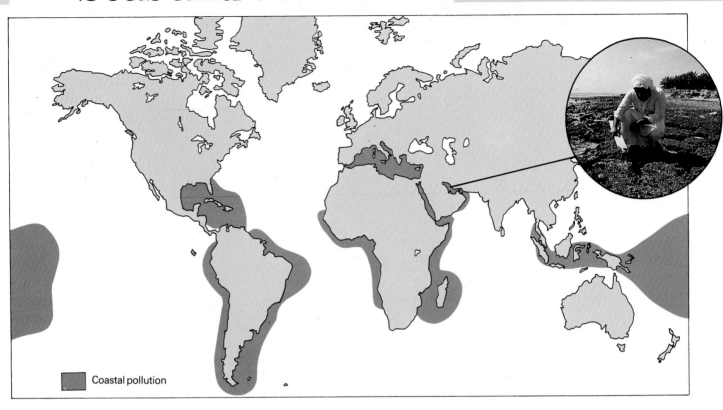

Coastal pollution

Seas and oceans cover more than seven tenths of the surface of our planet. They are so vast that you might think we could safely pour our wastes into their salty waters for ever, with no risk of damage. Billions of fishes swim in seas and oceans. You might believe that we could fish the seas for ever without using up these food stocks. On both counts you would be wrong.

Tainted seas
First, take the pollution problem. This century people pour more wastes than ever into seas and oceans. Most wastes run off the land into the rivers or are carried out to sea by winds. So inshore waters and shallow coastal seas suffer worst of all. The most heavily polluted areas include the Baltic Sea, the Mediterranean Sea, and parts of the Black Sea, Caribbean Sea and Bay of Bengal. Here, in places, fish and shellfish have died in great numbers.

Various man-made poisons are to blame. The commonest is sewage. This can suffocate sea creatures. Germs in sewage also make some beaches unsafe for bathers.

Spilled oil can coat shores in a sticky 'tar'. The United Kingdom listed over 500 oil spills in 1978 alone. Oil clogs seabirds' feathers. The birds preen, swallow oil and die from its effects. Thousands of birds perished from oil spilled by big sunken tankers like the *Torrey Canyon* and *Amoco Cádiz*.

Yet oil and also heavy metals mostly reach the sea from onshore refineries or smelting works. Poisons like mercury can build up in fishes' bodies, making some unfit to eat. In the 1960s many Japanese were paralyzed by eating contaminated shellfish. By the 1970s, Connecticut's oysters contained twice as much metal as they had in 1933.

Dangerous organochlorine and other pesticides have been washed off fields into the sea. In places like New York's Hudson estuary they build up in fishes' livers.

Saving the seas
Now, at last, the world is waking up to many of these dangers. In the 1970s, groups of nations agreed to stop dumping dangerous materials in their shallow seas. By the 1980s

▲
Nations are working to clean up these worst-polluted areas of sea. The inset photograph shows oil pollution in the Persian Gulf. In 1983 war-damaged oilfields leaked oil that killed off thousands of sea creatures.

▼
Shrimp-like krill swarm in some cold ocean surface waters. Eating krill might be one way of stepping up our food supply.

FISH CATCH (million tonnes)

Year labels on chart: 1979, 1978, 1977, 1976, 1975, 1974, 1973, 1972, 1971, 1970, 1965, 1960, 1955, 1950

Scale: 10 20 30 40 50 60 70

This diagram shows how the world's yearly fish catch increased, then levelled off. The world has yet to suffer the impact on fish stocks from dumping nuclear waste.

Shrinking shoals

Fish provide one of the world's most valuable supplies of protein food. To feed growing populations fishermen managed to treble the world's total fish catch between the years 1950 and 1970.

New fishing methods made this increase possible. Sonar devices, purse seine nets and factory ships helped fishermen to find, catch and process immense shoals of fish far from land.

Yet by the middle 1970s the world catch levelled out. Indeed some species were becoming scarcer — especially the North Atlantic's cod, haddock, halibut and herring. The reason was simple: people were catching the fish faster than the remaining fish could breed to make up the loss.

The same thing happened to the world's great whales. By the 1970s the blue whale — perhaps the largest beast that ever lived — seemed headed for certain

Dumping nuclear waste in the oceans may poison fishes and pollute the sea for thousands of years to come.

extinction. So did some other whales. Just in time, most fishing and whaling nations have agreed to stop catching threatened whales and fishes until their numbers can recover.

Some scientists believe we can increase the world's fish catch to meet the growing human population's need for extra food. To do this we may have to eat more of unfamiliar fishes such as kapelin, pollock and lantern fish — also squid and the shrimp-like krill. We shall also have to breed more fish and shellfish on fish farms.

All that might help us boost the annual seafood catch from 75 million tons in 1980 to 92.5 millions by the year 2000.

Even so, on average, each person will have fewer fish to eat.

deadly pesticides had begun to vanish from the seas off North America and north-west Europe. Also, oil companies were producing oil-eating bacteria and finding other ways of mopping up oil spilled at sea. New international laws should help to stop dangerous metals like mercury leaking into oceans.

Then, too, some countries are setting up marine national parks — special areas of offshore sea and seabed to be protected from all kinds of interference.

We can save the seas. But only if we closely watch and guard their health. Luckily, the seas now have a watchdog — the Regional Seas Programme of UNEP (the United Nations Environment.Programme). Scientists in this scheme check the purity of seas worldwide.

CHAPTER 4
The missing million

The world holds maybe five to ten million living species, mostly insects. But by AD 2000 a million species — many undiscovered — might become extinct.

Animals in danger

Many animals will go because people destroy forests and other habitats. But collectors and hunters might wipe out others.

By the early 1980s more than a thousand vertebrate species were on the danger list. There were fewer than a hundred Javan rhinoceroses. The California condor's numbers had dwindled to around fifty. Only two specimens of the Kauai O-O, a Hawaiian bird, survived.

Protecting threatened species matters more than many people realize. Some species could provide us with an extra source of food. Some are useful enemies of insect pests. Some poor countries rely on cash from tourists who come to see their wildlife. Then, too, the sheer marvel of how each creature's body works and suits it for its way of life deserves our wonder and respect. And, after all, each kind of wild animal has as much right to live upon the Earth as we do.

Saving the animals

What can we do to save the threatened creatures? The answer for those species with the fewest numbers is 'not much'. For those with several dozen individuals we can do more. Zoos and animal parks have bred beasts like the rare Arabian oryx and returned their multiplying young to suitable wild places where they are safe from interference. Governments protect some animals by setting land aside as nature reserves guarded by wardens to keep out hunters and collectors. Nations also band together to ban killing or collecting certain species.

Schemes like these began just in time to save the great whales and the Indian tiger. But more must happen to stop the list of threatened species growing.

Kakapo

Dodo

These animals have all suffered at the hands of man. The last dodo died three centuries ago. Père David's deer was barely saved. China's giant panda and New Zealand's kakapo seem headed for extinction. Tasmania's thylacine was thought extinct until one sighting in the early 1980s. Tree shrews are among the many creatures threatened as their forests disappear.

Père David's deer

Thylacine

Tree shrew

Giant panda

Vanishing plants

◄ Felling forests for firewood has bared Himalayan mountain slopes, now being washed away by rain.

► People's need for fuelwood destroys semi-desert plants right across Africa just south of the Sahara Desert.

▼ This map shows natural regions that most need protection from damage caused by over-use. High priority areas have no national parks to protect them. Priority areas have only small national parks.

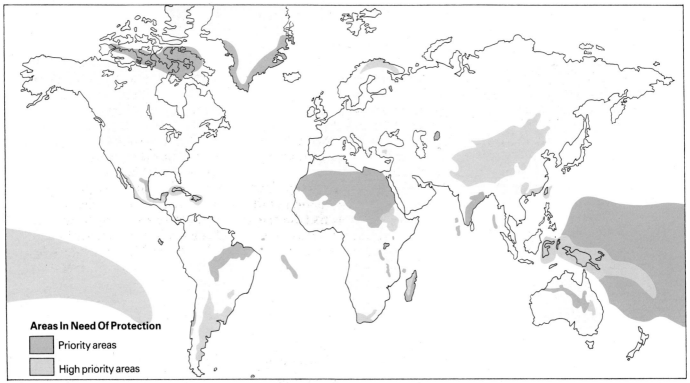

Areas In Need Of Protection

Priority areas

High priority areas

▲ Mangrove swamps vanish from muddy tropical shores as people chop down mangrove trees for fuel.

▲ Tropical forests almost everywhere are being felled or burnt at an alarming rate.

▲ Even Antarctica's bird life will not be safe if engineers move in to mine and drill for oil.

By the year 2000 scores of species of wild plant will have vanished. Experts think that 25 000, or one in ten, could go.

The plants most likely to be lost are species found only on small islands, or in the fast disappearing rainforests. The remote South Atlantic island of St Helena used to have more than a hundred kinds of plant found nowhere else. Only twenty still survive. More than 2000 unique plant species once flourished in the Hawaiian Islands. Over 200 have gone; 1100 more are threatened.

Why plants die out

Collectors are one important threat. They take rare orchids. They have put at risk that strange insect-eating plant the Venus flytrap, and Sumatra's stinking corpse lily, the world's largest, smelliest flower.

But plants are most at risk from loss of habitat. Between now and AD 2000, forest clearance in the tropics could help to destroy 137 species of plant and animal each day.

Loss of habitat also wipes out countless kinds of ancient food crops. At one time or another people have eaten at least 3000 plant species. But, bit by bit, they weeded out the least productive. Fewer than

▼
Wild barley yields small grains, but crossing this with cultivated barley could yield productive strains especially resistant to disease.

twenty species provide ninety per cent of all the food consumed today. Also, farmers have replaced thousands of old strains of wheat and rice with a few kinds that produce heavy crops.

Counting the cost

Letting wild plants and old crop strains die out could prove disastrous. Just think what we might lose.

Medicine uses ninety plants from Africa, Asia and Latin America. More than forty of these species grow only in the wild. Other plants yield products used in industry. Almost one third of the world's rubber comes from sap bled from the rubber tree.

Algin from brown seaweeds is used in soaps, shampoos, paints, dyes and other products. The jojoba bean from the deserts of north Mexico and the south-west United States produces oil suitable for lubricating car transmission systems.

There are probably many plants that could benefit us in ways we do not yet know — provided the plants survive. For instance, crossing a wild maize found in southern Mexico with a cultivated maize might yield a plant that grew corn every year like trees grow apples. That could do away with annual ploughing and sowing.

Crossing certain unproductive ancient strains of wheat or rice with modern forms can give strains

which produce high yields and are resistant to disease. Imagine what would happen with no old crop strains left to draw on. A new plant disease which could destroy the few strains that we cultivate today could starve the world to death!

Saving the plants

Saving every threatened plant is impossible. But botanical research stations can and do preserve thousands of old-fashioned strains of crops. For instance, the International Rice Research Institute in the Philippines keeps samples of an astonishing 45 000 strains of rice.

Also, nations set aside wild countryside as parks and reserves. Protected areas range from a tiny plot of ground where rare orchids grow in England, to Canada's Wood, Buffalo National Park, which is bigger than Denmark.

Not all these havens are safe from outside interference by miners, foresters or others. So conservationists try to persuade governments to leave untouched examples of every important kind of vegetation found on Earth.

The World Heritage Convention lists about 200 World Heritage Sites — those places in the world most deserving to be left just as they are. But only time will show if all survive.

▼
Euphorbias include some kinds of tree which produce hydrocarbons, the same ingredients that make oil such a useful fuel.

Wildlife invaders

While people are destroying thousands of species of wild plants and animals, some species actually profit by our activities. By design or chance, people are helping certain kinds to spread and multiply as never before. This happens particularly where we make it easy for wildlife invaders to move in.

Pests and weeds

By planting fields with certain crops, farmers provide vast larders for the animals and plants that thrive among or on cultivated vegetation. Before farming started, these pests and weeds were far scarcer than they are today. The same is true of pests and weeds in the garden.

Something similar takes place where woodmen chop down forests. Plants and animals that need light, airy, open spaces invade the clearings opened up by axe and chainsaw. In western Malaysia, grasses and banana plants move in on tracts of land cleared of the big trees that had kept the forest floor in shade. The new plants attract flocks of birds like yellow-vented bulbuls, and mammals like elephant, tapir, deer and gaur (a big wild ox).

In central Africa, mountain gorillas find lush feeding where primitive farmers have abandoned plots of land that they had cultivated in the forest.

Wildlife in cities

Wild plants and animals invade our cities too. After World War II, buddleia and willowherb bloomed among the bombed ruins of European cities.

Now, in North America, coyotes and raccoons scrounge food from city garbage cans at night. In Europe, red foxes prowl through city streets and gardens.

City buildings provide shelter for a whole zoo of animals — from dust mites too small for us to see, to mice and rats. In New York City, cockroaches feast on the plastic sheaths insulating the wires of television sets. London's window ledges make fine nesting sites for pigeons whose ancestors laid eggs on seaside cliffs. Parks and motorways can also provide refuge for plants and animals.

▲
The collared dove spread west through Europe this century. Man-made parks and fields of grain are to its liking.

► This bird's-eye view shows a raft of water hyacinth that chokes a water channel.

Across the oceans

Wild plants and creatures suited to our cities, farms and gardens just move in from the country around. But people help to spread some species all around the world, by ship or plane.

Ships have carried a giant kind of snail from Africa across the Indian and Pacific oceans to places where it does tremendous damage. By the 1950s 1300 kinds of insect — mostly stowaways — had reached the Hawaiian Islands and begun to breed. People freed a hundred European starlings in New York in 1890 and 1891. By 1943 these had produced 50 million descendants. They colonized the whole United States, and became fruit-pecking pests on farms.

Plant-lovers took the water hyacinth from South America all through the tropics. Now it chokes whole lakes and rivers with rafts of floating leaves.

The losers

Too often, plant and animal invaders wipe out native plants and animals by killing them or robbing them of food.

Sharp-toothed outsiders like the stoat and fox are destroying Australia's small native mammals. Lonely oceanic islands lose unique birds when ships land rats, cats, goats or pigs. These eat the eggs or kill adult birds of species that have lost the power to fly.

Animal invaders are driving into extinction up to one in five of all species of vertebrate (backboned) animal that disappear.

By the year 2000 we can be sure that pests and weeds and other hangers-on will be alive, well and multiplying. As fields and buildings replace woods and ponds we can expect to find more of those plants and animals that thrive among our farms and cities, and fewer of most other species. So wildlife will become less varied.

Luckily there are exceptions to this rule. Garden pools attract frogs, disappearing from the countryside as farmers fill in ponds and ditches. Garden trees and parts of gardens left untended will be wildlife havens too. Here at least some wild flowers and butterflies will still survive.

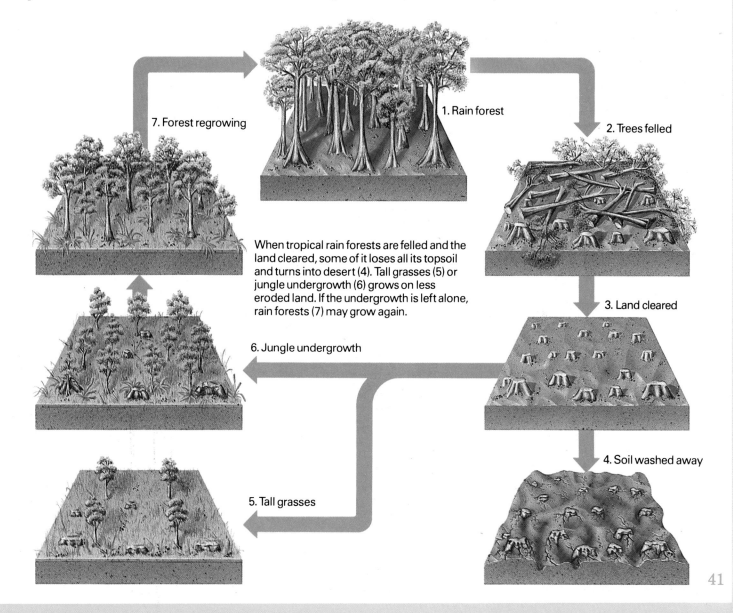

7. Forest regrowing

1. Rain forest

2. Trees felled

3. Land cleared

When tropical rain forests are felled and the land cleared, some of it loses all its topsoil and turns into desert (4). Tall grasses (5) or jungle undergrowth (6) grows on less eroded land. If the undergrowth is left alone, rain forests (7) may grow again.

6. Jungle undergrowth

4. Soil washed away

5. Tall grasses

41

CHAPTER 5
Search for substitutes

We should be plunged into a poor, Stone Age way of life if, all at once, we had no metals, coal or oil. In 1950 it seemed we should be mining these forever. Then came unexpected hints of shortages. This chapter shows why, and gives ideas for how we might overcome them to save our way of life.

The age of minerals

Civilization today owes much to what we mine. From minerals we get metals which are used in countless ways. For instance, aluminium is used in many vehicles and buildings. Iron is made into steel girders. We use lead in batteries, chromium in stainless steel, tin in cans, tungsten in the bits of drills. Then, too, oil is made into plastics, pesticides, detergents and chemical fertilizers.

Robbing the rocks

In the early 1970s experts calculated that many vital minerals, and the oil from which we get most plastics, might all be gone within a lifetime.

The results could range from inconvenient to horrifying. Take the loss of chromium for instance. We need this metal for oil refining, for producing rot-resistant steel and other vital purposes. No known element could take its place.

Luckily the worst forecasts have proved unduly gloomy. Technologists are finding ways to mine minerals from rocks where they are far from plentiful. Prospectors discover new sources of supply. Optimistic experts believe that there is much more aluminium and copper than the pessimists had calculated.

Even so, by the year 2000 some minerals will certainly be scarcer, more difficult to mine, and so more costly than today.

► Most plastic objects that we use are made of substances obtained from oil. When oil runs out our main supply of plastics disappears.

► In the middle 1970s experts worked out how long various useful minerals might last. Our diagram shows that several will disappear before the year 2000 if the growth in demand follows the predicted consumption rates.

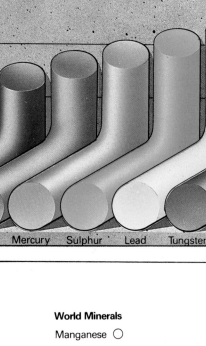

Silver · Zinc · Mercury · Sulphur · Lead · Tungsten

World Minerals

Manganese	○
Uranium	■
Iron	△
Aluminium	□
Gold	★
Zinc	☆
Silver	✕
Copper	◆
Lead	●
Tin	▲
Manganese nodules	⋮

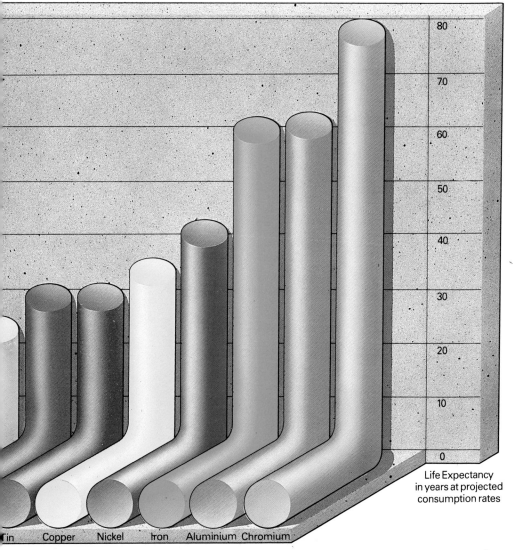

80

70

60

50

40

30

20

10

0

Life Expectancy
in years at projected
consumption rates

Tin Copper Nickel Iron Aluminium Chromium

Plastics from plants

One way of beating the shortage will be finding other substances to replace those in scarce supply. This is happening already. Scientists are learning that many of our plastic goods can be made as well from plants as they can from oil or coal.

Fossil fuels like coal and oil are hydrocarbons. Plants are mostly carbohydrates. The same chemical elements occur in each, in different arrangements. The main difference is that the hydrocarbons take millions of years to form, while carbohydrates occur in plants that grow in months. Some plants even yield two crops or more each year.

Sugar cane has already been used for more than sweetening drinks. Scientists are using cane sugar to make washing powders, soaps and cosmetic creams.

For thousands of years, people have turned sugar into alcohol with the help of tiny organisms called yeasts. By the year 2000, specially bred bacteria could turn sugar into raw materials for making plastics and synthetic fibres. These might replace those made from oil or coal.

▼
The world's main minerals including manganese modules, a rich source of manganese from the ocean beds.

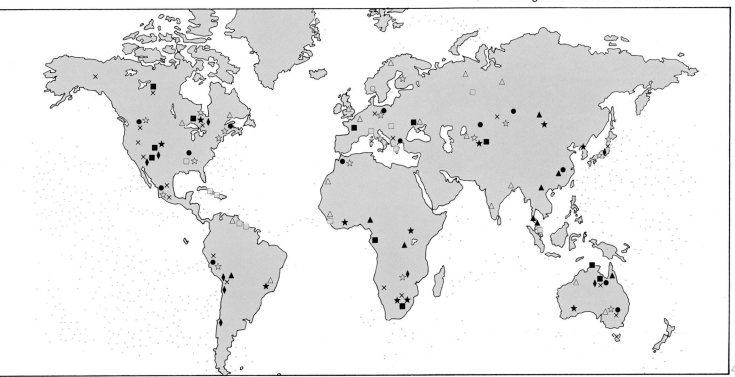

New ways of mining

As certain minerals grow scarcer engineers look for new ways of mining those that remain.

Microbe miners

One scheme is to make microbes do the work of men. By the next century, billions of bacteria too small to be seen could be toiling underground. These silent armies will tackle work now done by human miners to the roar of vast machines.

Already mining engineers are putting microbes to work, mostly on the surface. In Canada, South Africa and the United States, microbes help process rock already dug from vast open pits by giant mechanical shovels. The rocks contain copper or uranium but in such small quantities they are not worth extracting in the usual way.

Instead, sprinklers spray water on the piles of broken rock. The water picks up oxygen from the air and acids from the rocks that the water trickles through. This helps acid-loving bacteria to breed. Billions of *Thiobacillus* bacteria react with the rocks to produce iron sulphate and sulphuric acid.

Solutions of these compounds filter through the rocks, dissolving the minerals. Some of the minerals contain the metals copper, lead, uranium or vanadium. If a copper-rich solution then travels over scrap iron, the copper sticks to the iron. Scraping off the copper for collection is then easy.

Tomorrow's mines

In future, microbes could do much underground mining. This would work best for high-grade ores, that is rocks which are rich in metals. Microbes would dissolve the metals deep underground. Human miners would stay on the surface. Their task would be simply to control the pumps bringing up the metal-rich solutions to be processed.

Tomorrow's ore-extraction plants might look like today's water-treatment plants. There would be none of the ugly spoil heaps of ordinary mines.

► Manganese nodules can be collected from the ocean bed using remote-controlled robots (left) or they can be raked together and sucked up (right).

▼
Thiobacillus bacteria are used to extract copper from low-grade copper-ore. They are too small to see with the naked eye – these ones have been vastly magnified.

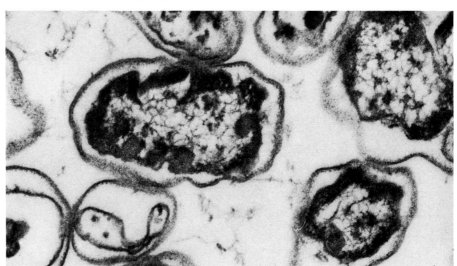

► Microbes extract copper from a copper-ore dump like this. 1 Sprinklers spray water on the dump. 2 Bacteria produce copper in solution. 3 Scrap iron removes the dissolved copper from the solution. 4 An oxidation pond removes unwanted iron from the solution. 5 A pump lifts the solution to the top of the dump for re-use.

Mining the seabed

On land we are fast using up supplies of valuable minerals. Yet so far we have scarcely tapped the riches deep beneath the sea.

It is true that much of our gas and oil comes from wells sunk in the beds of shallow seas. Also we dredge their floors for useful sands and gravels. But only now are nations turning to the deep floor of the open ocean for minerals which are soon likely to become scarce on land.

The richest prizes seem to be millions of manganese nodules — metallic lumps clustered most thickly over parts of the Pacific Ocean bed close to the Equator.

The nodules range in size from pebbles up to rocks that weigh a ton. They form when chemicals that were dissolved in sea water stick to fishes' teeth and other objects on the ocean floor. Nodules grow immensely slowly. Some take millions of years to add an inch (a few millimetres) to their thickness.

Besides manganese, the nodules contain such useful substances as aluminium, cobalt, copper, lead and nickel. What is more, nodules are accumulating metals faster than the rate at which we are consuming them on land.

To win these underwater riches we need new tools and know-how. By the late 1970s the American *Glomar Explorer* was the only ship capable of deep-sea mining. But several groups of companies now plan to raise metallic lumps from depths of 13000 feet (4000 metres) and more. The cost will be enormous, for deep-sea mining calls for a recovery ship to bring up the nodules, a fleet of vessels to ferry them to a coast, and an onshore refinery to extract the metals.

Already several schemes are in the making. Some nations will dredge nodules from the Pacific between Hawaii and Mexico. Others plan to mine the Indian Ocean and the seabed off New Zealand. Also, Saudi Arabia and the Sudan hope to bring up silver, zinc and copper from mud below the Red Sea.

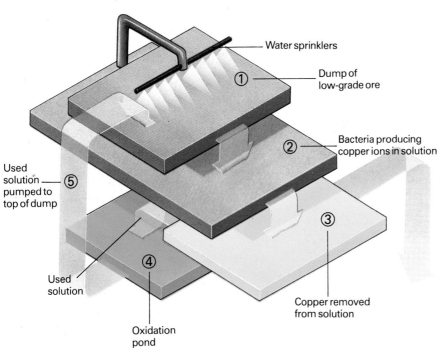

Water sprinklers

① Dump of low-grade ore

② Bacteria producing copper ions in solution

⑤ Used solution pumped to top of dump

③

④

Used solution

Copper removed from solution

Oxidation pond

The energy problem

Huge supplies of energy prop up our modern way of life. We need energy to cook food, to heat homes, to grow and harvest crops, to make manufactured goods, and to transport goods and people. Yet now comes the disturbing news that our energy supplies are running out. These pages show why and what will happen.

Energy guzzlers

The world's appetite for energy grew enormously this century. The amount of energy consumed rose by one third between 1970 and 1978 alone. But four fifths of this rise occurred in wealthy industrial countries. Business and industry tend to use 15 times more energy per head of population than in developing countries.

Rich and poor countries also use different fuels to provide them with energy. Poor countries burn mainly wood. Rich nations burn mostly oil, coal and natural gas. They also use nuclear energy and the energy released by falling water. These last five help to generate electricity.

Vanishing fuels

By the year 2000 the world will need even more energy than it does today. But experts reckon that the most heavily used sources of supply will be growing scarcer. For we are gobbling up coal, oil and natural gas faster than they are being formed.

Coal comes from the remains of ancient plants. Oil and natural gas form from the remains of other living things. All these fossil fuels have been hundreds of millions of years in the making. At the present rate, we might consume all world stocks in less than a hundred years.

Pessimists argue that by the year 2000 there will be too little oil satisfy demand. Optimists disagree. They think that we can squeeze out extra oil from oil shales and tar sands, and by drilling deeper offshore wells.

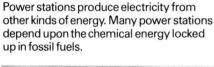

▼
Power stations produce electricity from other kinds of energy. Many power stations depend upon the chemical energy locked up in fossil fuels.

Milestones in energy use
(in the United States, the world's largest energy consumer)

1825 Natural gas is first used
1859 First oil well is opened
1885 Coal replaces wood as the main fuel
1947 Oil consumption overtakes production
1950 Coal replaces oil as the main fuel
1957 Nuclear energy starts producing electricity
1970 Oil production peaks
1973 Natural gas production peaks
1974 Cost of oil quadruples
1977 Formation of the Solar Energy Research Institute
1979 Nuclear accident stops the licensing of new nuclear power plants

---

Optimists argue that oil will last into the next century. They point out that we can also get oil from coal. A way of doing this already provides some of the oil used in South Africa. But using coal for making oil would simply speed up the rate at which our coal stocks would disappear. With care the world's coal could be made to last at least 230 years; but if we turn some into oil, coal might vanish in a century.

Natural gas will have an even shorter lifetime. At present rates, supplies will last no more than about fifty years.

Uranium supplies for nuclear power stations might dry up as fast as gas or oil. Building so-called breeder reactors could make uranium go a great deal farther. But their design gives many problems, and people fear that a nuclear accident could kill thousands. In the 1980s nuclear reactors became more expensive and governments found they needed less energy than they had thought, so fewer nuclear reactors than planned were built.

Fuelwood also faces a gloomy future. There has been a shortage since the 1970s. People have torn down trees for many miles around some towns just south of the Sahara Desert. No wonder some households spend up to 360 person-days each year just finding enough wood to burn.

As fuelwood disappears people burn dung and cornstalks instead, and so rob their soil of fertilizer.

Hydropower

Hydropower — electricity generated by the energy in falling water — may have a brighter future than other established energy supplies. More than one fifth of the world's electricity came from hydropower in 1972. Huge new hydropower plants were working by the 1980s, and there were plans to harness immense waterfalls in Africa and Asia.

Unlike fossil fuels, hydropower should last as long as rain fills the rivers. Yet hydropower has problems too. Power stations lose the force of the flowing water when the reservoirs that feed them begin to silt up.

Dodging disaster

If nothing takes the place of disappearing fuels, our homes will be hard to run, crop yields will slump, and factories and vehicles will fall idle. Millions of people will lose work, warmth and food, and die of cold or hunger. This need not happen.

As old energy supplies vanish new ones beckon, as the next four pages show.

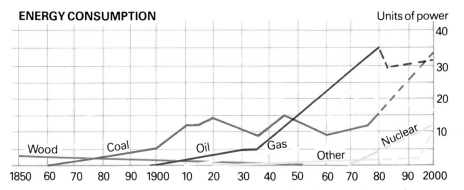

ENERGY CONSUMPTION

Units of power

40
30
20
10

Wood   Coal   Oil   Gas   Other   Nuclear

1850 60 70 80 90 1900 10 20 30 40 50 60 70 80 90 2000

▲ The amount of energy used in North America has increased rapidly in the last century. The type of fuel has also changed. Today very little wood is burned. Oil and coal supply most needs. In poorer countries, however, wood is still the main fuel.

◄ Dams pen back river water. Some let it spill through tunnels with great force. The energy in this falling water can be used for spinning turbines that produce electric current.

47

◄ Part of this house was built to trap heat from the Sun. Sunshine falling on large windows warms the rooms inside. Sunshine falling on solar panels helps heat the home's hot water.

► This wind turbine generates enough electricity to supply 2000 one-bar electric fires. The turbine stands on Block Island, off the east coast of the United States.

Once we have burned the world's supply of fossil fuels it will have gone for ever. Yet we shall never use up certain other kinds of energy. The Sun's rays will heat and light our planet for 4000 million years and more. As long as the Sun's heat sets the air in motion, winds will blow and waves will ruffle the oceans.

All we need are tools and techniques for trapping and using the energy in these renewable natural forces. These are by no means easy to find.

One of the main problems is that this energy is much less concentrated than the energy in coal or oil. Also, coal and oil hold stored-up energy that we can use at any time, whereas the energy in sunshine, wind or waves vanishes when the Sun sets, the wind drops or the waves subside.

Already, though, engineers are overcoming many of the difficulties. For example, take what is happening to harness solar energy or 'Sun power'. That source of energy is almost unbelievably immense. In one week the Earth receives as much energy from the Sun as the Earth contains locked up in all its stores of coal, oil, natural gas and uranium.

In sunny countries, millions of rooftop solar panels are now converting sunlight into heat for warming household water. As fossil fuels grow more costly, more people will use the Sun's free energy supply.

Sunlight can even generate electric current in two ways. One method uses mirrors to focus reflected sunlight on a tank or pipe to boil water that gives off enough steam to operate an electric generator. But such experimental solar power plants in the United States and France hold little promise of abundant cheap electric current.

Sunlight can also produce an electric current if it falls on a wafer of the substance known as silicon. Groups of silicon wafers can be used for making so-called photovoltaic cells. In sunny climates, arrays of cells are beginning to supply some villages with enough current to light lamps, pump water, and work a few household machines. Batteries help store up spare solar power for nights and cloudy days.

Soon, we might also see solar power plants in the sky. Above the atmosphere, solar cells would receive ten times more solar energy than here on Earth. Microwave transmitters would beam down that energy for use in cities outside the tropics.

The next three pages look at yet other ways of winning an almost endless supply of energy.

► Devices like the Clam convert the energy in waves into electric current. This test device was set up in a lake. The real thing would be far larger and tethered out to sea.

49

More energy supplies

Besides using the Sun's energy directly, engineers are inventing new devices to tap it second hand. These devices can harness winds, waves, and plants.

Putting wind to work

The world's winds release an unbelievable amount of energy. One calculation puts it at 100 million million megawatts. (The world's largest power station yields a mere 6000 megawatts.) People have put the wind to work for centuries, to power windmills and sailing ships. England alone contained 10000 windmills last century until steam engines took their place.

Now, though, new, more efficient kinds of windmill are being built around the world on windy coasts, hills and plains. These windpower generators look very different from the old windmills. Some have carbon-fibre blades, like giant aircraft propellers, controlled by microprocessors and mounted on tall concrete towers. By the early

1980s California had a huge aerogenerator able to produce three megawatts, enough current to operate 3000 one-bar electric fires.

Meanwhile Swedish scientists planned 3300 big aerogenerators. The Soviet Union aimed to build 150000 wind turbines by 1990. British scientists believed that arrays of aerogenerators off England's east coast could supply one fifth of Britain's electricity by the year 2000.

Storing the spare energy produced by aerogenerators can be done in several ways. Using that energy to recharge electric batteries is only one of them. You can also use it to pump water uphill to a storage lake. When the wind drops and the aerogenerator's blades stop turning you can switch on the batteries or let the water run downhill, spinning turbines to produce an electric current.

Of course wind can do more than just produce current. It can pump water, remove salt from sea water or

provide energy for air conditioning. Japan has even built a sail-assisted tanker.

One estimate suggests we could get seven times more energy from the world's winds than from the water in its rivers. If that proves true 'wind farms' of aerogenerators could be a common sight before the next century.

Harnessing the waves

Water already generates nearly one quarter of the world's electricity. Yet we harness only one fifth of all usable supplies. Soon, we could be using much, much more. Engineers have plans to capture some of the energy in ocean waves. Their targets include the rough seas around north-west and northern Europe. One British scheme involves the so-called Clam: a system of huge air bags mounted along a hollow concrete spine. Waves push the air bags in and out. This spins a turbine which generates electric current. But a big

Clam power station might need a stretch of coast 80 miles (130 kilometres) long.

Norwegian scientists are working on an alternative scheme. An underwater 'lens' would concentrate the waves and lift sea water into a reservoir. From there the water would fall and spin a turbine.

Yet other schemes use the daily surges of the tides to spin turbine blades. China, France and Russia already have tidal power stations. More are planned. One would put a vast concrete wall across the broad mouth of Britain's River Severn.

Firewood forests

Other promising supplies of 'endless energy' are biofuels — fuels obtained from living things. Many countries are planning to produce quick-growing crops that could be burnt directly, or turned into a gas or liquid fuel.

By early next century, poplar and willow plantations could

provide half of Sweden's energy. Ireland might plant forests of conifers, and hardwoods that could be mown repeatedly like grass. Philippine islanders are growing ipil-ipil trees yielding up to ten times more wood each year than pines do in cool climates.

Some euphorbias produce a kind of vegetable petroleum. The Japanese now tend 'petroleum plantations' on Okinawa Island. Americans, Brazilians, French and others are converting plant starches and sugars into ethanol (a form of alcohol) to replace petrol (gasoline) for use in cars. By 1983 nine in ten of Brazil's new cars ran on alcohol from crops like sugar cane. Soon, many countries will be producing alcohol for cars.

There is a snag, though. Land used for growing fuel is often land lost to growing food.

Other energy supplies

Even some non-renewable supplies of energy are almost limitless.

One scientist believes that vast supplies of methane gas lie trapped deep down in the Earth's crust. Also engineers are drilling holes to reach 'hot spots' in the crust and to use this heat for warming water.

But our best energy source could turn out to be hydrogen — one of the two ingredients in water. Scientists can 'split' water into oxygen and hydrogen gases. They can store hydrogen and burn it to heat and cool buildings or power cars. Hydrogen enthusiasts have begun to do all this in the United States.

Hydrogen atoms fusing together is what gives the Sun its energy. Scientists are trying to imitate that process here on Earth. If they succeed, controlled nuclear fusion would give us ample energy almost for ever. But no nuclear fusion plants are likely to operate before the next century.

◄ Brazilian pumps like this serve cars with alcohol instead of petrol (gasoline). Their fuel comes not from oil-wells but from huge plantations of the tall grass sugar cane.

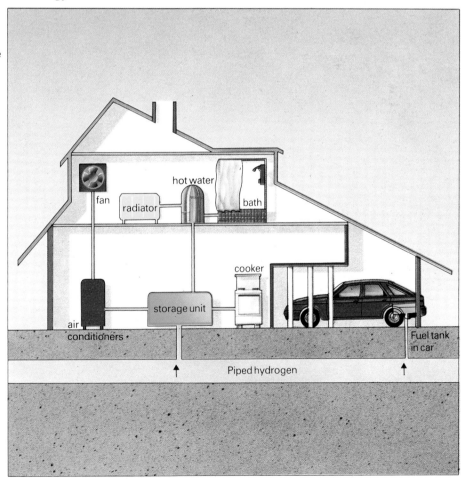

►This simplified diagram shows how piped hydrogen could serve as the fuel for cooling, heating, and cooking in tomorrow's homes. It could also fill a fuel tank in the family car.

CHAPTER 6
Making the most of it

Finding renewable substitutes for fossil fuels and some minerals will save us from some shortages. But we can make non-renewable supplies last much, much longer just by making better use of them.

Reusing garbage

While raw materials and fuels were cheap and plentiful we used them wastefully. Indeed we still do today. Articles like paper towels, aluminium food containers, and bottles are often made to be used once then thrown away; that is easier than washing articles for reuse later. Then, too, designers change the shapes of clothes and cars from year to year to make us buy new models to keep 'up to date'. So we get rid of goods because they are old fashioned, not because they are worn out. That wastes huge quantities of useful substances and the energy that went into making them.

The garbage produced by our throw-away style of life creates a vast disposal problem. The United States sets land aside for many thousands of garbage dumps. Their total area is as big as Rhode Island, the smallest US state.

Reusing materials can bring huge benefits by saving the fuels required to manufacture them, and by saving the substances which will soon be in short supply. Changing old newspapers into new paper or cardboard saves nearly one quarter of the energy needed to make paper from wood. Saving a ton of paper also spares twelve trees from the woodman's axe.

Recycling scrap steel saves nearly half the energy used in making steel from iron ore. Reusing aluminium needs a mere 4 per cent of the energy required for making aluminium from its ore. If the United States reused all bottles, every year it would conserve 5 million tons of glass, 1.5 million tons of steel (by using fewer cans), 0.5 million tons of aluminium, and up to 46 million barrels of oil.

'Save it' schemes already operate in many countries. People sort out waste paper, glass or metals for collection. In 1978 Japan recycled three times more waste than back in 1974. Japan now reuses nearly half of all its garbage. By the year 2000 more industrial countries will almost certainly do likewise. By then, today's throw-away society may be a memory.

Saving energy

We waste huge quantities of energy. When coal is burnt in homes less than a third of its energy is used. Much of the rest escapes up the chimney. Similarly, power stations lose more than half the energy in the fuels they burn in order to produce electricity.

Making more efficient use of energy could cut down sharply the quantities of fuel we need. As oil and coal become more costly, people have begun to realize it pays to do just that.

Better insulation is bringing huge fuel savings. Lagging hot-water tanks, walls, floors and roofs can halve the amount of heat that leaks from our houses.

If gadgets like water heaters and air conditioners were designed to be more efficient, the United States could save the equivalent of over 4000 million barrels of oil by early next century.

Saving fuel

Huge savings are appearing in transport too. Cars are being made with new, streamlined shapes to cheat the wind. New controls help car engines to make more efficient use of fuel. Such changes can halve the amount of fuel they use. Drivers save still more fuel by living near their work or by sharing cars with passengers.

Already, 'save it' schemes are having an effect. In the early 1970s the United States seemed set to guzzle energy at a rapidly increasing rate well into the next century; now the future looks quite different. Some Americans expect their country to consume far less energy in the year 2000 than it used in 1979.

▼
Many cities are beginning schemes to recycle their garbage rather than just dumping it all.

Metals such as aluminium, lead and tin can be melted down and used again.

This bottle bank sorts out bottles according to the colour of glass – green, brown, and clear. The glass is crushed, melted and reused.

Collecting and reusing rags can bring riches. Rags can be made into high quality paper. Woollen rags can be reused for making woollen clothes.

Cities make, sell and then throw away millions of newspapers each day. They can be repulped and made into cardboard, or brown paper, or used again as newsprint.

Conservation

Many of the 'save it' benefits just mentioned will come from cities. But the countryside has much to offer, too. For instance, in many poor countries, just cooking over stoves instead of open fires would save nearly half of all wood burnt.

Protecting soil

For farmers, soil itself is the most valuable resource of all. An inch or two of soil takes centuries to form, yet the wrong farming methods can destroy some soils in less than a dozen years.

Conserving soil is often easy. One way is by ploughing across a slope instead of up and down. Rainwater then sinks down into the furrows instead of washing soil away downhill. Techniques like this could protect the nearly two fifths of the United States farmland which now loses five tons of soil or more per acre every year. That nation and many more would benefit from national plans to save soils most at risk.

Organic farming

Tractors, chemical fertilizers and chemical insecticides and herbicides use vast amounts of oil-based energy. We could save much of this if farmers used organic, 'natural', substitutes.

A few Western farmers have gone back to ploughing land with horses instead of tractors. Horses multiply themselves, and their droppings provide more natural fertilizers than the kinds that come in sacks from factories. But horses do need valuable land to grow the grass they need to eat.

Other farmers stick to modern farm machines and modern types of seed; but they use animal manure and keep down the weeds without chemical pesticides. They simply plough and plant at times the weeds dislike. Also they grow different kinds of crop on the same field in different years.

This is called crop rotation and it helps to keep the soil fertile.

New ways with pests

Pesticides kill insects that eat the crops. There is no doubt that we could save much of the oil energy now used for making pesticides.

Poor countries are already learning to use pesticides more sparingly. Small farmers spray crops carefully by hand from cylinders of pesticide strapped on their backs. This is less wasteful than spraying crops by tractor or by aircraft.

But as pests become resistant to some pesticides, farmers are forced to spray ever bigger doses. Often this kills bees and other useful insects that pollinate the flowers to produce all kinds of fruits. In time, though, some pests may grow so resistant to a pesticide that it no longer works on them. This happened in the 1950s in Peru's Cañete Valley. Insect pests which had become completely resistant to man-made insecticides destroyed half the cotton crop.

Scientists solved this problem with simple commonsense. They timed cotton planting and planned cotton growth in ways the insect pests disliked. Just by not growing cotton on the same ground every year they left too little time for the pests' numbers to build up dangerously. The experts also brought in insect predators to eat the pests. Such measures more than doubled the cotton crop.

Scientists now know of many 'friendly' viruses, bacteria and fungi that attack specific pests. Such microscopic allies could help to replace pesticides. Certainly, using nature in this way would help to save half the crops that pests destroy today.

In short, 'natural' farming methods produce good harvests.

◀ This can be a much better way of spraying crops than using a tractor, aeroplane or helicopter (right). Hand sprays do not waste so much of the expensive chemical pesticides, and they can be concentrated where they are needed, on the affected crops, rather than covering everything in their path.

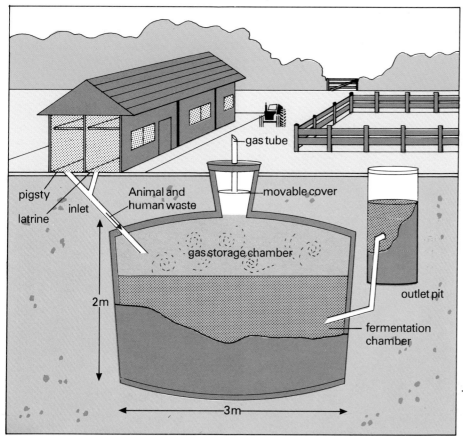

pigsty
latrine
inlet
gas tube
Animal and human waste
movable cover
gas storage chamber
outlet pit
2m
fermentation chamber
3m

They conserve soil better than ordinary modern methods, and use far less fuel. As oil-based energy grows scarce, organic farming will help us make the most of croplands.

Fuels from farmyards

Farmyard manure can be more than just organic fertilizer. It can also be burnt as a fuel. Some farmers ferment cow, pig, chicken or even human manure in an airtight digester. The stuff yields methane gas which can be burnt for heating or for powering vehicles and farm machinery.

By the time this book appears, China may have 70 million methane digesters. Cattle manure alone could supply nearly one fifth of the natural gas used in the United States. Farmyard fuels surely have a very useful future.

◄Methane digesters convert animal and human waste into methane gas which can be used to heat the home or to drive tractors and other farm machinery.

Feast or famine?

For more than 17 centuries, Maya Indians multiplied in Guatemala. Suddenly, a thousand years ago, nine tenths of their population disappeared. Scientists believe that their increasing population overused the soil. Then soil erosion cut crop yields. Many thousands may have starved. Now only empty ruins show where Maya centres buzzed with life.

Spaceship Earth

To save our own civilization we must learn to see our planet as a spaceship speeding through an empty sky. Like astronauts we must make very careful use of everything our craft provides, for that is all we have. And like astronauts we must be careful how we dispose of waste. There is a limit to what our world can take and still stay healthy.

Unhappily, many people are too busy grabbing what they can to see the problems this will bring upon themselves. In some poor countries, a few big landowners exploit the underfed, landless masses. Similarly, rich nations jealously guard their wealth and let their Third World trading partners struggle to avoid starvation. Without land reforms in certain countries, and more equal trading partnerships between nations, discontent will breed wars and revolutions. And if great nations start fighting over dwindling natural resources, nuclear weapons could wipe civilization off the world map. The few survivors could slump into a miserable Stone Age kind of life.

No one wants this. So self-interest, if nothing else, should bring the changes that will help our world survive. Already there are hopeful signs.

Planning for change

Governments are beginning to make people change their ways of life to meet our planet's future needs. Governments can do this in several ways. They can simply give us information and advice. President Carter took such action

WORLD POPULATION (Millions)

[Graph showing world population from 1970 to 2020, y-axis from 3000 to 6000]

If every country does its best to limit population growth, the best we can hope for is that world population will not rise above 6000 million before the year 2020.

▼

Vast amounts of money are spent on war planes, tanks and weapons. If this money was used to protect and conserve the countryside, we might see some startling changes by the year 2000. Family-planning programmes could be improved and

when he urged Americans to turn down thermostats in winter and up in summer — to save fuel used in heating and air-conditioning their homes.

Governments can also pass laws forbidding drivers to exceed a certain speed. (Not driving fast saves gasoline/petrol.) Government

rewards and penalties include items such as grants to help people pay for insulating their homes, and high petrol taxes that discourage drivers from buying big fuel-guzzling cars.

'Save it' and similar schemes will work only if we curb our population growth. Not long ago this seemed impossible. Numbers rose fast in the 1970s. In 1980 the human population passed 4400 millions. In the early 1980s, an extra million people were born every five days.

Yet now at last come signs of slowing down. Rich industrial nations show the lowest rate of increase. At late 1970s rates of growth, Western Europe's population would take nearly seven centuries to double. Yet population still soars in the poorer tropics. By AD 2000 there may well be twice as many Africans as there were in 1977. But things are very different

perhaps halt the increase in population. Semi-deserts could be reclaimed and felled forests replanted with trees. Much of the sea and air could be made pollution free.

in China, which has nearly one quarter of the world's population. By AD 2003, China's population may show no growth at all. That incredible achievement would come from government rewards and penalties aimed at persuading parents to have no more than one child per family.

Besides governments, various international organizations strive to save our world in one way or another. Branches of the United Nations Organization keep a watch on items like world food supply, and the health of oceans. The World Wildlife Fund (WWF) and the International Union for Conservation of Nature and Natural Resources (IUCN) are two groups that work to help the threatened wildlife of the world.

With aid from other groups, in 1980 IUCN produced *World Conservation Strategy*. This major scheme shows how and why saving wild plants and animals will help protect mankind from hunger.

What we can do

Governments and international groups help to shape the future. But in the end it is largely up to us — each one of us — to make the world a cleaner, safer place to live in by the next century, and there is much we can do. We can help in simple ways like collecting and sorting household scrap to be reused. We can discuss conservation problems at school and we can write to politicians about them. We can have fewer children than our ancestors did. We can join organizations that work to save our planet from misuse. Above all we can elect governments prepared to plan for the long-term good of people everywhere.

► To us the Earth seems huge, but to an astronaut looking down from Space our planet looks much smaller and more fragile – and it is the only place we know where life can exist. We must protect and conserve the resources we have.

Glossary

Acid rain Rain made acid by chemical pollution of the air, especially by factories, power stations, cars and trucks.

Aerogenerator A modern type of windmill designed for generating electricity.

Asteroid Any of thousands of lumps of rock circling the Sun. The largest measures as far across as the British Isles.

Atmosphere Gases surrounding a star or planet. The Earth's atmosphere consists of the mixture of gases called air.

Bacteria Microscopic organisms sometimes grouped with plants.

Biofuels Fuels obtained from plants or animals. Wood, ethanol (ethyl alcohol), and methane from manure are three examples.

Biosphere The part of the Earth that contains living things. It includes the lower atmosphere, the waters and the upper crust.

Breeder reactor Nuclear power plant that produces more nuclear fuel than it consumes. It changes a form of uranium into a form of plutonium.

Carbohydrates Chemical compounds made of carbon, hydrogen and oxygen. They include sugars, starch and cellulose. Plants and animals need carbohydrates for their living processes.

Carbon dioxide A gas made of carbon and oxygen atoms. Air contains tiny quantities. Plants use it for making carbohydrates.

Carbon-fibre A strong type of fibre made by heating textile fibres. It adds strength to some glass, plastics and ceramics.

Cellulose The main ingredient in the cell walls of plants. Cellulose is a tough, fibrous substance.

Clam One device for using the mechanical energy in waves to generate electric current.

Climate The usual type of weather of a given place, measured over many years.

Compounds Substances each made of two or more elements that are chemically combined.

Croplands Lands used for growing crops, especially crops that people eat, or feed to cattle, pigs or chickens.

Crust The solid surface of the Earth. It consists of a thin skin of soil and a layer of solid rock several miles deep.

Cycle A number of events that lead back to the point where they started.

Deforestation Clearing land of forest.

Desert Land so dry that little vegetation grows there.

Detergents Cleansing substances, including washing-up liquids.

Elements Substances made entirely of one kind of atom.

Energy The power to do work. One kind of energy can be changed into another. For instance, the chemical energy in coal can produce heat energy and heat energy can produce electrical energy.

Ethanol Ethyl alcohol: a kind of alcohol obtained by fermenting fruits, grains, vegetables etc. It can be used instead of petrol, or mixed with it to make gasohol.

Fertilizers Plant foods. Natural fertilizer or manure includes animal droppings and rotted plants. Artificial or chemical fertilizer includes nitrates made in factories.

Fish farms Ponds where people raise fish until these are big enough to be eaten.

Fluorocarbons Chemicals containing fluorine and carbon and used in refrigerators and canned sprays. They tend to destroy ozone in the upper atmosphere.

Fossil fuels Fuels made of or produced by the remains of prehistoric plants or very tiny prehistoric organisms. The main fossil fuels are coal, oil and natural gas.

Fuels Substances that can be used to produce heat energy.

Fungi Plant-like organisms that feed on dead or living matter. They include mushrooms, moulds, smuts and yeasts.

Genes Tiny structures in the cells that make up living things. Genes determine how cells develop. Different genes control different inherited features among plants and animals.

Geneticists Scientists who study the natural laws that decide what a plant or animal inherits from its parents.

Greenhouse effect The way in which carbon dioxide traps the Sun's energy and is warming up the surface of the Earth.

Heavy metals Metals that can poison if absorbed by the body in more than very tiny amounts. They include lead, cadmium, mercury, beryllium and nickel.

Herbicides Poisons used to kill weeds.

Hydrocarbons Chemical compounds containing only the elements hydrogen and carbon.

Hydrogen A light, invisible gas that can be burnt as fuel, but is dangerously explosive. On Earth most hydrogen is chemically combined with other elements.

Hydrogen fusion The joining of hydrogen nuclei — the 'cores' of hydrogen atoms. Hydrogen fusion releases vast amounts of energy.

Hydropower Electricity produced by the energy in moving water. It is also called hydroelectricity.

Ice Age A long, cold spell in Earth's history, when ice caps spread from the polar regions.

Ice caps Huge, thick, masses of ice. Ice caps cover most of Antarctica and Greenland.

Industrial nations Nations that earn money largely from factories that turn raw materials into finished products.

Insecticides Poisons that kill insect pests.

International Union for Conservation of Nature and Natural Resources (IUCN) This organization publishes lists of endangered species. It also suggests which are most worth saving and how to go about it.

Irrigation Watering land to provide crops with moisture.

Manganese nodules Ores found as lumps on the deep ocean floor.

Manure See **fertilizers.**

Methane The main ingredient in natural gas. Methane is obtained from natural gas trapped underground, or by fermenting manure. It can be burnt as fuel.

Microwave transmitters Transmitters that beam out energy in the form of invisible microwave radiation.

Minerals Rocks with certain chemical ingredients. (Fossil fuels are not true minerals.)

Mites Insect-like creatures with eight legs. Some are too tiny to be seen. Some feed on plants, others feed on animals.

Modern Man Our own species: *Homo sapiens* ('wise man'). This species was evolving by 200 000 years ago. People just like us appeared by 40 000 years ago.

Natural gas See **methane.**

Nature reserves Lands set aside to protect wild plants and animals. Many are known as wildlife parks. The world has thousands but many are tiny.

New World The Americas.

Nitrates Certain compounds containing nitrogen. Nitrates are valuable plant foods.

Nitrogen A colourless, odourless gas. Nitrogen is the main ingredient in air. Combined with other substances it can form **nitrates.**

Nomadic peoples Wandering peoples. Most are herdsmen or shepherds. Many roam the fringes of deserts or wander on mountains. They seek seasonal pasture for their herds and flocks.

Non-renewable resources These are useful things like ores and fossil fuels that cannot be replaced once used up.

Nuclear power plant A set of buildings using nuclear energy to produce electricity. The nuclei or 'cores' of uranium or plutonium atoms split to give off heat and other kinds of energy. The heat is used to spin turbine blades and so produces electric current. Nuclear power plants are also called nuclear reactors.

Oil shales Dark, soft rocks containing hydrocarbons. Quarrying and heating the rocks releases oil. There are huge oil-shale deposits in some parts of the Rocky Mountains.

Old World Europe, Asia and Africa.

Ores Minerals containing useful amounts of metals.

Organic farming Farming based on 'natural' methods like using animal manure instead of artificial fertilizer.

Oxygen A colourless, odourless gas. Oxygen is the second most plentiful ingredient in air. Plants and animals need oxygen to stay alive.

Ozone A form of oxygen found high in the atmosphere. It shields us from most of the Sun's ultraviolet radiation.

Pesticides See **herbicides** and **insecticides.**

Pests Plants or animals that harm people or their crops or animals. Where one kind of crop or farm animal abounds, so do the pests that feed upon it.

Photochemical haze A smog-like haze produced by sunlight acting on nitrogen oxide gas given off by car exhausts.

Photovoltaic cells Devices that directly convert sunlight into electricity. Thousands of these cells produce only enough electricity to heat a one-bar electric fire.

Polar Regions The world's cold Far North and Far South, around the North and South Poles.

Pollution The poisoning or dirtying of air, land or water by impurities.

Purse-seine nets Huge fishing nets that can be pulled shut to trap a shoal of fish.

Radioactive waste Waste from nuclear fuels and certain other substances. These give off energy as invisible rays and/or particles. Much radiation leaking into air, soil or water can harm living plants and animals.

Rainforest Forest found in rainy climates. Tropical rainforest has more plant and animal species than any other kind of place.

Rangelands The grasslands of the world, where people graze sheep and cattle.

Raw materials Substances from which we get useful finished products. For example iron ore is a raw material used in making steel knives and forks.

Recycling Reusing waste paper, metal, glass and so on.

Renewable energy supplies Energy supplies that cannot be used up — for instance sunshine, wind, waves and rivers.

Reservoirs Man-made lakes used to store water for irrigating crops or supplying water to homes and factories.

Roughage Coarse, bulky food rich in plant fibres.

Smog Fog containing dust, soot, and choking sulphur dioxide.

Soil Particles of broken rock mixed with decayed plant and animal matter, air and water. Soil provides plants with a roothold and nourishment.

Solar cells See **photovoltaic cells**.

Solar energy The energy in sunshine.

Solar panels Glass or plastic panels behind which water flows over black metal surfaces that absorb heat from the Sun. The units form solar collectors. Many warm water in homes.

Solar power plant A group of mirrors that concentrate the Sun's heat to boil water. The steam generates electricity.

Sonar A device using echoes to 'see' fish shoals or underwater obstacles. Its name is short for Sound Navigation Ranging.

Species This is the smallest important grouping of related plants or animals.

Stone Age The three million years or so before people learnt to make metal tools. Old Stone Age people were hunters and food gatherers. New Stone Age people farmed and kept food animals. The New Stone Age was developing 10000 years ago. In places it lasted only about 5000 years.

Sulphur dioxide A colourless gas with a choking smell.

Tar sands Layered rocks with billions of tiny holes that trap sticky oil deposits. There are big deposits in the Canadian province of Alberta and in the American state of Texas.

Third World A name often used for the world's poor nations, mostly found in the tropics.

Tidal power station A power plant using tides to spin turbine blades to generate electricity. It is also called a tidal barrage.

Tropics The world's hottest regions. They lie on either side of the Equator, an imaginary line around the Earth's centre.

Ultraviolet rays A type of invisible energy from the Sun.

United Nations An international organization formed to help nations work together for peace and prosperity.

United Nations Environment Programme (UNEP) This is an international scheme to check the health of the world's air, land and water. Its scientists warn of pollution, overfishing and other dangers.

Upright Man *Homo erectus* This ancestor of modern man appeared about two million years ago and survived for over one and a half million years.

Uranium A radioactive element used as fuel in nuclear power plants (nuclear reactors).

Vertebrates Animals with a backbone — fishes, amphibians, reptiles, birds and mammals.

Viruses Minute infectious organisms. They invade and feed on larger living things, causing disease and even death.

Volcanic eruption An outpouring of hot gases, dust and/or molten rock from a volcano.

Weeds Wild plants that compete with cultivated plants for air, light, soil and moisture.

Wetlands Swamps, marshes and other places that are damp or under very shallow water.

World Heritage Sites These are unique natural and cultural places valuable as part of the heritage of people everywhere. The World Heritage Fund helps to pay for the World Heritage Convention whose member countries work to protect their own sites.

World Wildlife Fund An international organization for protecting wildlife around the world. It raises cash to buy land for nature reserves or to pay for their protection, etc.

Index

Picture acknowledgements

Heather Angel/Biofotos 38 bottom left, 40
right, 62 top **Camerapix Hutchison** 25, 50
right, 52-53, 54 **Bruce Coleman Limited**
16, 20 bottom, 34 bottom, 36 top, 36 bottom,
37 top, 37 bottom left, 37 right, 38 top left, 38
bottom centre, 39 left, 40 left, 48, 55, 58
bottom, 62 bottom **Daily Telegraph Colour
Library** 23 bottom, 38 bottom right, 52, 53
left **Earthscan** 26 **The Mansell Collection**
36 centre **Rex Features** 34 top, 56 **Science
Photo Library** 31, 49 top, 57 **Sea-
Lanchester Wave Energy Group** 49
bottom **Frank Spooner Pictures** 53 centre
Tupperware 42 **Vautier-de Nanxe** 50 left
Vision International 10-11, 53 right
**Westfälisches Amt für Denkmalplege,
Munster** 29 **ZEFA** 46

Artwork by **Mulkern Rutherford** and **John
Strange**.

Multimedia Publications (UK) Limited have
endeavoured to observe the legal
requirements with regard to the suppliers of
photographic and illustrative materials.